The Personal Wellness Principles

Simple Steps to Create a Happy, Healthy, and Fulfilling Life

JOHN M. BROS

Published by

JIII PUBLISHING CO

TREASURE COAST, FL

ISBN: 978-0-578-75059-0

Cover and interior by Gary A. Rosenberg
www.thebookcouple.com

*This book is dedicated to
the Bros and Bova families.*

Each person must discover his own philosophy of life, and it is not fair or right to impose our codes upon others. It is also our responsibility, however, to share one with another such experiences as may have common value.

We desire, therefore, not to convert or convince, but to invite such a sharing with the sincere hope that some mutual good will be accomplished.

—MANLY PALMER HALL

Contents

Preface

In the summer of 2017, I began pondering various principles of life that I was using in an effort to become a happier and more centered person. A friend encouraged me to convey these themes in a book, so that others could also benefit. I immediately thought of my dad's work, a book he published under a pseudonym in the early 2000s entitled *P*, which recognized the positive effects of various "P" words—like *passion, purpose,* and *poise.* These principles were directly related to the success of the human experience—and similar to the ideas I wanted to convey. So I decided to use some of his principles as a guide to creating my vision—and *The Personal Wellness Principles* was born, as an amplification, elaboration, and extension of my father's work.

As a kid, I wasn't necessarily ready to understand the themes and lessons of my father's original work, but as I've gotten older, I recognize their significance. This recognition inspired me to write *The Personal Wellness Principles,* in hopes of encouraging and positively influencing people to pursue and maximize their own personal wellness.

The Personal Wellness Principles is intended not as a one-time read, but as a guide to daily practice—read and applied little by little to help the reader attain new pinnacles of personal wellness. This is a self-help book that contains thoughts, concepts, and perceptions intended to help the reader develop, advance, and apply the various principles. In each chapter, you'll find an introduction to the "P" principle, followed by a hands-on exercise, "Practicing Your Principles," which will help you apply that principle in your life. At the end of each chapter, you'll find a collection of quotes related to the principle, meant to inspire and encourage you.

Committing to self-growth means you believe you have the power and control to improve, develop, and enhance your life, and that you know you are the only one with the ability to set that process in motion. It is my sincere hope that *The Personal Wellness Principles* improves your quality of life and that of anyone else who reads it, guiding you toward self-awareness and growth to the greatest version of yourself you can be.

1. Discover Your Passion

Find a job you enjoy doing, and you will
never have to work a day in your life.
—MARK TWAIN

Passion is any powerful and positive emotion that gives meaning to life, such as love, joy, happiness, and bliss. Passion takes many forms, from interests, ambitions, and goals, to the love people show for friends and family. If you're not living to your fullest levels of achievement and happiness, then you're probably not exercising your passion(s) to the best of your ability. To bring forth your passion(s) means to live in a fulfilled and completed state of being.

For example, a friend of mine tried to learn how to ride a horse but fell off several times. Naturally disappointed, she quit because she felt like a failure. When she tried to learn how to ice skate, she fell even more. But this time, she didn't quit, as she'd been captivated by the elegance of figure skating and the incredible attention to detail that it required. Even though she could have allowed herself to feel like a failure in this undertaking as well, she had a different perspective about ice skating because it made her feel alive. When she realized this, she knew it was her passion and worth pursuing.

Characteristics of Passion

When you have passion, an intense driving force motivates you to do these things:

1. Be involved with the things you're passionate about as much as possible.

2. Persevere toward a goal.

3. Take chances.

4. Sacrifice short-term discomfort for long-term prosperity.

5. Strive for the next level of improvement.

Passion can also have the following effects on you:

1. You truly love the time you spend doing the things you're passionate about. There is nothing else you would rather be doing, even if your achievement level is low.

2. You're energetic, and your enthusiasm inspires others.

Creatives like artists, musicians, and dancers are naturally passionate people. For instance, passion is important when creating a great song. When vocalists have a passion for the lyrics they write, that passion comes through in their voice. When other members of the band sense and feel the emotion a vocalist puts into lyrics, then they in turn express themselves through energetic and passionate solos and music. The passion that one group of musicians or dancers shows inspires the next wave of young people who want to feel and emulate the passion they see in the creative expression of the musicians and artists they look up to.

Perhaps you went to school to become a doctor because your parents encouraged you toward that profession. Maybe you spent 12+ years of your life learning, researching, and working with content that really didn't excite you. Maybe you ended up with a $200,000+ salary because of all that work, allowing for luxury and extravagance. But what if, after all that time, energy, and money spent on higher education—what if after all of that, you still weren't happy?

A state of unhappiness after achieving such high accolades would indicate that inside your heart and soul, you knew there was something else you'd rather be doing. The good news is, it's never too late to make profound changes in your life that will permit you to follow *YOUR* passion and path. As author Stephen Cope states in his book *The Great Work of Your Life* (2012), "People actually feel happiest and most fulfilled when meeting the challenge of their dharma [passion] in the world, when bringing highly concentrated effort to some compelling activity for which they have a true calling . . . . Fulfillment happens not in retreat from the world, but in advance—and profound engagement." When you commit yourself *entirely* to your passions, personal wellness can manifest in your life more freely.

The Difference Between Passion and Obsession

At times, you may be unable to control your passions, leading you into destructive behavior and decision-making. This is when passions become obsessions, when something has a level of priority in your life that doesn't deserve the amount of energy you're giving it. When you're obsessive, you lack the ability to think logically and responsibly. You may spend so much time and energy on one thing that you lose sight of the things that really matter—like your own personal growth and development, which are directly related to your personal wellness and well-being.

I see a lot of this during football season, when the most important thing in the world for many of my friends is the time from Thursday night until early Tuesday morning—the time spent watching as much football-related entertainment as possible. Whether it's time spent organizing fantasy football teams, time spent online making bets with bookies, or the actual visual consumption of football on television, it's the singular constant on their minds. When their fantasy team loses or they lose bets, they inevitably descend into negativity, anger, and unpleasantness. When their passion causes their overall happiness to decrease significantly, or even causes them to lose money, then their passion has become an obsession.

Don't let your passion turn into obsession. Do what you love without letting it control you, and you'll enjoy the benefits of good health and happiness.

Practicing Your Principles

Reflect on the various things in your life that give you meaning and enthusiastic energy. Make a list of five things that are, or could be, passions of yours. Then begin incorporating those passions into your daily life as frequently as possible. You can start by prioritizing your list and beginning with Passion Number One, then adding others as time allows. But remember, don't allow any of them to become obsessions.

Note: If you want to go deeply into the pursuit of passion, I recommend you read *The Passion Test* (2006) by Janet Bray Attwood and Chris Attwood.

Words of the Wise about Passion

*"When equal talents collide,
passion decides the victor."*

—UNKNOWN

"You can do anything as long as you have the passion, the drive, the focus, and the support."

—SABRINA BRYAN

"A great leader's courage to fulfill his vision comes from passion, not position."

—JOHN MAXWELL

"Chase your passion, not your pension."
—DENIS WAITLEY

*"Chase down your passion like it's
the last bus of the night."*
—TERRI GUILLEMETS

*"Passion is born when you catch a
glimpse of your true potential."*
—FRED SMITH

*"Only passions, great passions, can
elevate the soul to great things."*
—DENIS DIDEROT

*"Your passion is waiting for your
courage to catch up."*
—ISABELLE LAFLÈCHE

*"Follow your own passion—not your
parents', not your teachers'—yours."*
—ROBERT BALLARD

*"If you feel like there's something out there
that you're supposed to be doing, if you have a
passion for it, then stop wishing and just do it."*
—WANDA SYKES

"I would rather die of passion than of boredom."
—VINCENT VAN GOGH

"If you can't figure out your purpose, figure out your passion. For your passion will lead you right into your purpose."
—BISHOP T.D. JAKES

2. Learn from the Past

Don't let the past ruin your future.

—MANLY P. HALL

The father and founder of Taoism, Lao Tzu, proclaimed: "If you are depressed, you are living in the past. If you are anxious, you are living in the future. If you are at peace, you are living in the present."

How often do we live in the moment, in the immediate present? "Not often enough" is the only honest reply. Many people live in the past, unable to adapt to the present moment for whatever reason. Perhaps they're living in the glory days of yesteryear, or maybe they're focused on something negative that happened to them and refuse to move on so they can focus on the present.

But the advice to "learn from the past" is a reminder that you cannot change anything that's happened to you, right up to this exact moment. Instances that make us regret our past are impossible to go back to, and those events will never again happen exactly the way they did so we can have a do-over. So don't dwell on past negative experiences—it will only waste your energy and time by causing you continued pain, stress, and sickness.

When you make a mistake or fail, or when something doesn't go as planned, don't sulk and wallow in self-pity. Rather, learn from the mistake, apply that new knowledge in the future, and move on in a positive direction.

Learn from *All* Past Experience

Keep in mind that dwelling on a *positive* experience can also be an unproductive practice if it means constantly reliving the past rather than moving forward with your life. People want so badly to relive great experiences and emotions. But even this is a form of living in the past and is thus unhealthy. Those former experiences and emotions may be nice memories, but use them for motivation—don't allow them to own you or prevent you from flourishing in the present and moving forward.

For example, for a period of time after college in my early twenties, I was unable to move on with my life because I spent my time living in the past. I had moved to Thailand in the fall of 2014 to teach English at a top Thai high school called Mahidol Wittayanusorn. Overall, it was an unforgettable experience, one that was imperative for my self-growth.

While I was there, I met a woman from the United States who was also teaching, just a few hours from my school. We ended up dating. Then, in July 2015, I took a job teaching in Florida and moved back to the States. She was still in Thailand, however, and over time, our relationship became strained and things came to an end.

It upset me for longer than I'd like to admit. I lived in the past for quite a while after that. I *chose* to live and think in the past rather than adjusting to the present and moving forward. I eventually realized that the only reason we had met was to help each other grow and develop during that time spent abroad. I decided that the purpose of every relationship is to help learn and grow from one another for as long as it lasts, whether it's six months or six years. It wasn't up to me to understand why it ended; rather, I needed to be thankful for my time spent with her in the past, and to be OK with the fact that it was over.

Sometimes, forgetting the past means cutting off certain friendships and relationships that have become toxic and overly negative. Cutting out a friend or significant other due to their toxicity is a brave step toward personal wellness, but with this often come the aftereffects of loneliness and grief. Be confident and steadfast with your decision; don't allow yourself to reconnect with toxic people just because you feel lonely at times. Trust that you made the right choice and that the current isolation you feel allows space to attract better people into your life who deserve your time, energy, and friendship.

Now, some people do just the opposite of living in the past: they instead focus excessively on the future, on things that haven't yet occurred. Don't allow thoughts about your future to paralyze you in the present moment, which you should be cherishing. Being prepared and properly planning for life is a well-regarded quality, but there's a difference between planning for the future and creating stress and problems out of thin air because of things that don't exist or haven't happened. Planning for the future is a positive until it negatively affects the present.

Of course, there are those like Lao Tzu, those who have trained their minds to live in the present—*now*. They choose to learn from their past and look to the future with wonder and hope for the greatness to come. Most importantly, they recognize the present moment as the most precious thing we will ever have.

Escaping the Prison of the Past

Sometimes, people ignore or deny an incident from their past. They either hope the memory of it will go away, or they are unable to come to terms with and accept whatever negative thing happened. But however upsetting experiences and memories from the past may be, they don't magically disappear by pushing them aside and refusing to acknowledge them. In many cases, suppression of emotions and memories leads to bigger problems later on. Therefore, in order to help you move on with your life, you have to recognize and confront the past. No matter the discomfort, no matter the embarrassment you allow yourself to feel—which is just your own ego at work—you have to face the problems of the past in order to live a fruitful future.

Here's how Arlene (not her real name) did this. Arlene's daughter died unexpectedly after a neurological complication she had from taking an unknown substance at a concert. In the middle of the concert, she had a severe seizure from a drug she'd been given, and she died shortly thereafter. For a long time, the devastation and pain caused by the unexpected death of her daughter made Arlene incapable of living her life. She didn't eat, she didn't sleep, and she no longer went to her job.

After some time, she realized she needed to make a drastic change. She knew that her daughter wouldn't want her living this way, and she longed to find a new sense of purpose while dealing with the trauma of her daughter's death. And she found it: speaking to teenagers about what happened to her daughter to help them avoid falling into the same situation.

Arlene created an emotional presentation, sharing her story with students at various high schools across school districts in the southern United States. She viewed this new sense of purpose as her own special duty, bestowed upon her to help prevent others from experiencing her tragedy. This new sense of purpose not only has a positive impact on the kids she speaks to, but it also allows Arlene to cope with her devastating loss, battling the pain of her past by neutralizing its negative energy in the present.

It is important to learn from the past and move on, rather than waste time fighting change and circumstances. Some people become permanent prisoners of their past, unable to see all of the opportunity for greatness in front of them at the present moment. The past is meant for one thing, and that is to learn lessons; it is *not* meant to hold you hostage as your own mental prisoner. If you spend your whole life with regrets, wishing you'd done things differently, then you will never be conscious of the opportunities and experiences available to you at this exact moment. Make peace with your past; you owe it to yourself to move on with a clear mind and heart. In the words of Shakespeare's Macbeth, "What's done is done." Choose to no longer regret the past, to no longer fear the future, to be bold and live only in the ever-present now.

Practicing Your Principles

Be honest with yourself and search internally for three things from your past that continue to limit you in the present. They could include a failed relationship you focus on too often, a missed once-in-a-lifetime investment opportunity, or regret from missing out on a great party or trip with friends. Pick one and ask yourself what you can do to help yourself let go of that issue. Talk it over with a friend? Read a book on self-forgiveness? Anything from the past that you still hold negativity toward—find it, come to terms with it, and move on from it.

WORDS OF THE WISE
ABOUT THE PAST

"Stop being a prisoner of your past.
Become the architect of your future."
—ROBIN S. SHARMA

"The past has no power over the present moment."
—ECKHART TOLLE

"You can victimize yourself by wallowing
around in your own past."
—WAYNE DYER

*"The past can't hurt you anymore,
not unless you let it."*
—ALAN MOORE

*"I'm looking forward to the future,
and feeling grateful for the past."*
—MIKE ROWE

*"The past cannot be changed.
The future is yet in your power."*
—MARY PICKFORD

*"I pray that former rejection and deep hurts
will not color what I see and hear now."*
—SUE AUGUSTINE

*"The past should be learning experience
and not an eternal punishment."*
—NUTHAN POOJARI

*"Losers live in the past.
Winners learn from the past."*
—DENIS WAITLEY

"The more anger toward the past you carry in your heart, the less capable you are of loving in the present."
—BARBARA DE ANGELIS

"Never look back unless you are planning to go that way."
—HENRY DAVID THOREAU

"It's good to leave each day behind, like flowing water, free of sadness. Yesterday is gone and its tale told. Today new seeds are growing."
—RUMI

"The secret of health for both mind and body is not to mourn for the past, not to worry about the future, or not to anticipate troubles, but to live in the present moment wisely and earnestly."
—SIDDHARTHA GAUTAMA, THE BUDDHA

3. Practice Patience

Patience is bitter, but its fruit is sweet.

—ARISTOTLE

Patience is the ability to accept delay, interruption, or aggravation without complaining or becoming angry. It is the capacity to calmly endure during times of frustration. To be patient, you must be able to control your reactions to various situations and inconveniences.

It's impossible to practice patience, or apply it in life, without consciously recognizing the plethora of knee-jerk reactions we have to the inconveniences we face daily. Achieving patience is an *active* process—not a passive, random happening. In other words, unless you're naturally an incredibly patient person, it requires mindfulness to learn patience.

How I Learned Patience

Before moving to Thailand, I was told the pace of life there would be much slower than what I was used to in the States. The nonstop working pace of Western life was different from the slower-paced lifestyle of the Thais. To travel on the weekends, I had to take a bus from my town to Bangkok, where I was then faced with the stressful task of looking for the correct taxi van area—marked in Thai writing (which I can't read)—where I would find a van to take me to wherever I was going.

On my first weekend trip, I got to Bangkok safely, found the taxi depot with vans to the town where I was going to visit a friend, and bought my ticket. According to my ticket, we were scheduled to leave at 7:00 p.m. and arrive by 9:00 p.m.

But we didn't leave at 7:00 p.m. Five minutes turned into ten, then ten minutes turned into twenty, and I began to become very impatient—what was my driver thinking? He was sitting on a stool, peeling an orange, acting like he wasn't working and that we weren't late. I began to get very annoyed, and I was pretty angry at the whole situation. But at some point, I looked around and realized I was the only one who seemed bothered by all this inconvenience. All the other Thais in the van with me acted as if nothing was wrong.

A college student who was on my bus sensed how bothered I was and felt compelled to practice his English. He told me that "everything was OK" and that the driver "was just hungry." We left by 7:30 p.m., and I couldn't help feeling a certain level of shame and embarrassment that I'd reacted the way I had. It wasn't an inconvenience for anyone in the van except me.

I realized how much practice I had ahead of me if I were ever going to attain the level of patience and composure the other passengers maintained. When we got to our destination, the driver dropped us off in a shopping complex parking lot. I had absolutely no clue how to find my friend's apartment complex in the town, but the young man who had spoken to me earlier told me his mom was picking him up and that they would be more than happy to take me to the apartment complex I had mentioned. Sure enough, they took me straight there. I thanked them profusely, and we enjoyed the unique moment together. Their level of selflessness and compassion made a lasting impact on me, as did the lessons of patience I learned that day.

Ways to Practice Patience

Every day, people are given the chance to practice patience on their way home from work. No matter where in the world people are working, when it gets to the clock-out time of the day, they have the same general reaction: *Finally, I can go home!* They start their vehicle, turn on their a/c (or heater), and eventually, pull their car onto the road, that much closer to their beloved couch, pet, and significant other. Everything is going fine until they see the standstill, bumper-to-bumper traffic ahead.

At this point, most become impatient or angry. And we know that some may even become violent, depending on their level of road rage.

What if, rather than beeping at one another or angrily and dangerously trying to switch lanes to get ahead an extra 100 feet, we took that time stuck in traffic to reflect on and ponder about our day? To think about the things we had learned that day that offered us opportunities for growth because they had either helped us or hurt us. That time in the car could be used to call loved ones or friends to catch up. The time could be used to listen to music we love, an audio book, or podcasts that cover an array of topics. The point is that the same time spent sitting in traffic feeling angry and aggressive could be used to do any number of other things—*if* we chose to practice patience.

Most people today know of Bruce Lee's outstanding martial arts abilities—but few are aware of his wisdom, philosophy, and calculated life. One of his best known quotes is, "The most dangerous person is the one who listens, thinks, and observes." What does he mean by this? Typically, when we hear the word *dangerous,* we automatically assume that physical well-being and safety are at risk. But Bruce Lee isn't referring to danger in the physical sense; he's referring to becoming great in one's mental ability and capability—becoming a mental warrior, if you will. Bruce Lee is telling people to *speak less* and *listen more.* The more we listen, the more we think; the more we think, the more we observe; the more we observe, the more capable we are of relating to others and growing our minds.

Speak less, listen more, and be conscious of the importance patience plays in your personal wellness.

Practicing Your Principles

Your ability to be patient and control your reactions to unpleasantness is one of the most important abilities you can develop. Practicing patience takes work, and like anything, you will have to be objective in your search for it. Be observant of your reactions to inconveniences. The next time you feel your temperature rising, take a breath and see if you can separate yourself from the unpleasantness of the situation by focusing on something else for a moment.

Multiple times per week, reflect and try to identify a time when you could've been more patient with someone. *At the same time*, identify a time when you were especially patient and acknowledge the great work you're doing in this area.

WORDS OF THE WISE ABOUT PATIENCE

"Patience, persistence, and perspiration make an unbeatable combination for success."
—NAPOLEON HILL

"Have patience. All things are difficult before they become easy."
—SAADI

"The two most powerful warriors are patience and time."
—LEO TOLSTOY

"Patience is not the ability to wait, but the ability to keep a good attitude while waiting."
—JOYCE MEYER

"Adopt the pace of nature: her secret is patience."
—RALPH WALDO EMERSON

"Genius is patience."
—ISAAC NEWTON

"Be patient and understanding. Life is too short to be vengeful or malicious."
—PHILLIPS BROOKS

"The test of good manners is to be patient with the bad ones."
—SOLOMON IBN GABIROL

"Patience and perseverance have a magical effect before which difficulties disappear and obstacles vanish."
—JOHN QUINCY ADAMS

"Two things define you: your patience when you have nothing and your attitude when you have everything."
—GEORGE BERNARD SHAW

"Patience is when you're supposed to get mad, but you choose to understand."
—UNKNOWN

"To lose patience is to lose the battle."
—MAHATMA GANDHI

"Patience is the calm acceptance that things can happen in a different order than the one you have in your mind."

—DAVID G. ALLEN

"Patience attracts happiness; it brings near that which is far."

—SWAHILI PROVERB

"I have just three things to teach: simplicity, patience, compassion. These three are your greatest treasures."

—LAO TZU

4. Pay the Price

Let the rest do whatever, while you do whatever it takes.

—GRANT CARDONE

When you "pay the price," it means that you have the courage to make sacrifices that will positively affect your personal wellness. Generally, such sacrifice is in relation to achieving a goal or completing a task that you've set. Paying the price requires the fortitude to work when no one else is working, to plan when no one else is planning, and to ponder when no one else is exercising their brain.

Paying the price means you must set aside any and all notions of instant gratification and instead place *incredible* focus and energy on achieving what you seek. Doing this can ultimately manifest success, self-improvement, and happiness.

Let me share a couple of examples. To win a game, some athletes are willing to pay the price with their bodies. For instance, many hockey players choose to lie in front of an opposing player's shot, purposely trying to block a puck traveling at 100 mph, the damage of which can range from shattered jaws and orbital bones to broken ankles, depending on where the puck hits. Another example is a

23

quarterback who waits until the last second to make the perfect pass, getting crushed by a huge hit in the process because of the patience that was necessary to make the play. Perhaps that blocked hockey shot helped lead the team to a Stanley Cup, or the QB's perfect pass was the Super Bowl–winning touchdown; both are good examples of paying the price.

As a young kid, I was a bit overweight, which made it really tough growing up in a place like South Florida, where pool parties, boat outings, and beach trips were always prevalent. I always kept my shirt on and couldn't enjoy myself because I was so self-conscious. It affected me all the way through the age of 18. But as a freshman in college, I decided enough was enough and that I was going to change the conditions in my life. I knew that I was going to have to pay the price physically if I wanted to finally see improvements in my health and in my body.

Initially, these sacrifices were not easy, as I felt vulnerable and in way over my head. I had to start from a completely blank slate, taking anything I thought I knew about nutrition and health and throwing it out the window. I wanted to know everything, from how to properly read and evaluate nutrition labels, to learning new perspectives on *real* food and how to use it as fuel intended to aid my body. I applied this new knowledge to my life and started eating and thinking differently. I committed to working out every day of the week in one capacity or another, whether it was jumping rope, lifting weights, swimming, or playing hockey.

As the weight came off and I saw improvements, I was encouraged and motivated to keep moving forward.

Since then, fitness and health have become top priorities in my life because I know how vital they are for my personal wellness.

A friend of mine had a goal that she would earn a 4.0 GPA in college. Toward the end of her senior year, she was faced with a conundrum that would require her to pay the price. An opportunity came up toward the end of the spring semester to take a scuba diving trip to the Bahamas. But if she went to the Bahamas, she would miss the final days of her teaching internship, which could possibly affect her letter grade and the final score she would receive for her internship. She was disappointed to miss the trip, but she chose to stay.

It turned out to be the right decision, as her evaluator passed her with high marks and comments that not only sealed the deal in her achieving her 4.0 GPA, but also secured a job for herself at that *same* school she interned at after she graduated. Although she missed the Bahamas trip, she positioned herself to have a job she's not only passionate about, but that now allows her to go to the Bahamas with her family every summer.

Sacrifice Is Its Own Reward

The current sociocultural climate in much of the Western world is one of excessive and unnecessary reward systems, accompanied by the incessant need for instant gratification. People want to be handed everything on a silver platter, without presenting any of their own willingness to put in the work and energy needed to accomplish their vision. Everyone wants change, whether it's change in their inner life, change at work, or change in their marriage, relationships, and friendships; however, very few people are *willing TO change.*

It isn't enough to wish for change—you *are* the change that you're willing to produce and emit into your environment. You are only going to ascend to your greatest self if you're willing to pay the price and make change when it's necessary. It takes a very brave person to pick themselves up and realize that all they desire and wish to attain is solely up to them, that the sacrifices they make and their own willingness to pay the price along the journey are all that stand between them and their ultimate vision.

This theme of paying the price also includes understanding when the time has come to move on from certain friends, family, or significant others, which we touched on briefly in Chapter 2. The fear of cutting toxic people out of your life comes not from the thought of those people being out of view—after all, that is the end goal. Rather, the crippling fear comes from the realization that with change comes discomfort. Whether or not that discomfort is temporary or eternal is up to you.

Most are afraid to make the changes they yearn for because they know that with change comes a period when the familiarity and comforts of consistency disappear. Consistency is indeed a comfort, but it is also an illusion. This illusion produces a laziness and complacency, which allows mistreatment experienced by others to be perceived as OK. People endure maltreatment from a person because they fear living life without the familiarity and security associated with that person, not because of the person's character. So pay the price of temporary discomfort *now* to find the people who will support you, motivate you, and love you in the future.

How far you go in life is entirely up to you. You must accept the premise that life will at times be painful, discomforting, and inconsistent with what you desire. But when you acknowledge that *you* are the one who's in control of your life and future, it becomes much easier to accept that temporary discomfort, difficulty, and struggle just add up to the price you must pay in order to discover what you ultimately seek. As William J. H. Boetcker said, "The difficulties and struggles of today are but the price we must pay for the accomplishments and victories of tomorrow."

Practicing Your Principles

Concentrate, reflect, and try to find something in your life that you feel you could be doing better in—like a facet of your job, or your health, or an area of your schooling. Look for areas of life that bring you pleasure, such as watching sports or scrolling through social media, and just for a day, keep track of the time you spend on those activities. Acknowledge that you may need to sacrifice some of the time you spend on those pleasures to correct the other areas of life that need more focus. Try also to focus on a life goal that you want to achieve so badly that you're willing to surrender other areas of your life that take up time in order to achieve your ultimate vision.

WORDS OF THE WISE
ABOUT PAYING THE PRICE

"Nature cannot be tricked or cheated. She will give up to you the object of your struggles only after you have paid her price."
—NAPOLEON HILL

"Problems are the price you pay for progress."
—BRANCH RICKEY

"Scars are the price you pay for success."
—MELVIN VAN PEEBLES

"What you have become is the price you paid to get what you used to want."
—MIGNON MCLAUGHLIN

"The speed of your success is limited only by your dedication and what you're willing to sacrifice."
—NATHAN W. MORRIS

"Everything you do in life causes the effects that you experience—when you get the bill, be prepared to pay."
—IYANLA VANZANT

"Greatness doesn't come at a discount.
If you want true greatness, you have
to pay the full price for it."
—DAMILOLA OLUWATOYINBO

"One of the principle things life has taught
me is that we always have a choice. When
we say 'can't,' we usually mean we're
just not willing to pay the price."
—PATRICIA MCCONNELL

"The most important decision about your goals
is not what you're willing to do to achieve
them, but what you are willing to give up."
—DAVE RAMSEY

5. Perpetuate Happiness

There is no path to happiness.
Happiness itself is the path.

—A. J. MUSTE

Perpetuating happiness should be a priority in every-one's life, as it directly correlates to your personal wellness. To accomplish this, you must make a conscious effort to maintain happiness *whenever possible.* Of course, realistically, everyone's happiness fluctuates from time to time, depending on the happenings in their life. But the goal is to experience a high level of happiness—such as joy and elation—in all of your days.

Even indifference is OK as long as you're neutral and don't allow your perspective to reach toward the negative side of things. And achieving this state of mind should never come at the expense of becoming selfish or neglecting responsibilities. To be conscious of your happiness means you possess an overall awareness that allows you to move on from brief disappointment and to *make the choice* that disappointments and hardships won't keep you down for long.

Perpetuating happiness doesn't mean you have to be smiling and elated at all times, nor is this a reasonable expectation. But it does mean that a state of happiness is always right around the corner or waiting to be re-attained. Understand that at any given moment, you can either have feelings of sadness or feelings of happiness. The emotions you convey depend on which perspective *you* choose, and because of this, happiness is relative to each individual. What makes one person happy or indifferent might make another person sad, and the feelings you have today could very well be different tomorrow.

Sadness caused by the death of someone close to you is one of the most difficult experiences to overcome, but you can conquer it. You have the power to choose how you want to approach this or any other tragedy you inevitably will face during your life. I'm not saying you can magically click your heels and everything will be fine—you may suffer unimaginable pain when you lose someone close to you, and it's something you'll have to experience in order to fully understand. However, after that initial pain and shock, you can make the choice not to allow it to control your future thoughts, emotions, and actions. Eventually, you can choose to be thankful for the time spent with that special person and for the lessons learned from them, in order to regain happiness rather than spend negative energy, time, and emotion feeling sorry that they're gone.

Routine and ritual help to perpetuate happiness and increase personal wellness. For some, this may include daily allotments of meditation, prayer, or concentration. Meditation silences the mind, prayer connects people to their higher power, and concentration projects the focused mind into a vision of the goals people want to manifest for themselves. Other examples of routine and ritual may look more like having a weight training and stretching routine or dedicating a part of the week to playing sports and seeing friends.

Ask yourself, am I happy? If the answer is yes, then that's great and you should keep doing whatever it is you're doing. However, if you're not happy, then it should now be evident to you that some type of positive change must immediately happen in your life so you can rediscover happiness. That change may be dietary, or it may require moving, getting a new job, getting into shape, practicing gratitude more (see Chapter 14), or even volunteering your time to a higher cause. Whatever it may be, if you're not happy, you need to make immediate changes.

Habits of the Happiest

Below are guidelines to help you maintain or restart your happiness:

1. Wake up every day and proclaim out loud, "I'm glad to be alive, and I will choose to be happy and well today!"

2. Say or write the five things you're most thankful for in your life at that moment.

3. Be productive with a meaningful hobby or interest. For example, start an organic garden and learn how to grow a variety of nutritious and nourishing fruits, vegetables, and spices.

4. Persevere. Understand that roadblocks and negatives should not bring sadness; they are a part of life.

5. Participate in various group activities.

6. Always give more than you take.

7. Engage in your passions and purposes daily.

8. Laugh daily and enjoy some form of art, such as listening to music, drawing, or dancing.

9. When you feel sad, ask yourself, Is it worth having this feeling dominate my emotions and take away my happiness? Adapt and adjust.

10. Ignore the negative hearsay people may repeat about you.

11. Learn new skills to become wiser and to keep life fresh.

12. Be philanthropic with your time and money by doing something nice as a surprise for somebody. It doesn't have to be big and expensive to make a profoundly positive impact on someone's day, and it doesn't have to be for someone you know.

13. Meditate and/or pray, depending on your personal beliefs.

14. Be attentive to diet, exercise, and sleep.

15. Before you go to sleep for the night, reflect on all of the great things in your life and ponder the possibilities of a new tomorrow.

Practicing Your Principles

Read over the Habits of the Happiest in this chapter again. Which are you applying, and which do you need to work harder at? Do your best to apply all of the habits throughout your week.

Words of the Wise
about Perpetual Happiness

*"The best way to cheer yourself
is to try to cheer someone else up."*
—MARK TWAIN

*"Don't cry because it's over, smile
because it happened."*
—LUDWIG JACOBOWSKI

*"For every minute you are angry, you
lose sixty seconds of happiness."*
—RALPH WALDO EMERSON

*"Happiness is when what you think, what
you say, and what you do are in harmony."*
—MAHATMA GANDHI

"No medicine cures what happiness cannot."
—GABRIEL GARCIA MARQUEZ

*"Three grand essentials to happiness in
this life are something to do, something
to love, and something to hope for."*
—JOSEPH ADDISON

*"Happiness isn't getting what you want,
it's wanting what you have."*
—GARTH BROOKS

*"True happiness arises, in the first place,
from the enjoyment of one's self."*
—JOSEPH ADDISON

*"Be happy for this moment. This
moment is your life."*
—OMAR KHAYYAM

*"Folks are usually about as happy as
they make their minds up to be."*
—ABRAHAM LINCOLN

*"The secret of happiness is not found
in seeking more, but in developing
the capacity to enjoy less."*
—SOCRATES

*"A wise man is content with his lot,
whatever it may be, without wishing
for what he has not."*
—SENECA

"Be content with what you have; rejoice in the way things are—when you realize there is nothing lacking, the whole world belongs to you."

—LAO TZU

"Happiness is like a butterfly; the more you chase it, the more it will elude you, but if you turn your attention to other things, it will come and sit softly on your shoulder."

—HENRY DAVID THOREAU

"Happy people build their inner world... unhappy people blame their outer world."

—T. HARV EKER

"The man who makes everything that leads to happiness depend upon himself, and not upon other men, has adopted the very best plan for living happily."

—PLATO

6. Be Persistent

Ambition is the path to success.
Persistence is the vehicle you arrive in.

—BILL BRADLEY

Persistence is the ability to stick with something, to continue forward despite adversity, and to acquire a "never-give-up" attitude. In short, persistence is unhindered tenacity. This never-give-up attitude can be used to achieve professional goals, to attain personal goals, and to complete necessary tasks, big or small.

Persistence requires strong mental fortitude, a positive mental state, and the courage to conquer temporary disappointments, in order to attain your ultimate vision. To be persistent means picking yourself up every time you get knocked down, moving forward and adapting to all complications, and realizing that all disappointments and trials are but momentary roadblocks on the way to what you seek.

Persistence depends on the following qualities:

1. Willingness

2. Dedication

3. Courage

4. Ability to not take things personally

When people are persistent, they make the *choice* never to allow failure to stop them; they possess the confidence to help them achieve any goal or vision they set, despite adversity. Even when faced with hopelessness, impossibility, and despair, they are *willing* to keep going and to trust their path.

The first test of the new school year leaves some high school students happy and some disappointed. The most likely reason the disappointed students didn't score as well as they'd liked is that they didn't prepare well enough. In that moment of frustration, however, those students can either continue to be upset and sulk in their disappointment, or they can acknowledge the need to make a change. After all, something is only a failure if they choose not to learn from the mistakes that led to this "failure." Through this realization, students begin to understand the only way to succeed is through persistent *dedication* and preparation to their studies.

Courage is also paramount to people's persistence. When things don't come easy, the human spirit can be broken, and if people aren't careful, their hardships and misfortunes will consume them and blur their visions and goals.

Finally, persistent people understand that criticisms are nothing to take *personally*; rather, they are something to learn from. Criticism is one of life's sharpest double-edged swords. When people receive honest criticism from friends, family, or esteemed colleagues, they have the choice either to benefit from this critique or to take it personally. Criticism allows open-minded people to see their work/life/purpose from a different angle, and as a result, enact the necessary change to become their best. This choice in perspective is the difference between people who want to experience personal growth, self-progression, and ultimately, personal wellness, and people who take everything personally, refusing the help, guidance, and suggestions of those around them.

Persistence is paramount to personal wellness because it means maintaining a mindset that is open to progress and development, as opposed to a mindset that is shut off from outside influence, fixed in its ways, and certain that "things are just the way they are." Persistent people understand that strenuous effort, when directed and executed properly, is the only way to self-mastery. For every great creation, invention, and conception, there are loads of previous attempts and efforts at the same undertakings that were not well rewarded, that failed, that people scoffed at; yet, we live in a world of absolute wonder due to the persistence of those who didn't allow setbacks to keep them from reaching their final destination.

Practicing Your Principles

Being persistent in times of hardship is one of the most important things you can train yourself to do. Roadblocks can make you or break you. Want to be able to finish what you started? Want to see things through to their completion? Take the phrases "I quit" and "I give up" out of your vocabulary. If you find yourself about to give up, see if you can change your language to something like, "I'm going to take a break to regroup; then I'll try this again."

WORDS OF THE WISE
ABOUT PERSISTENCE

*"Great starts are not as important
as great finishes."*

—UNKNOWN

"If at first you don't succeed, try, try again."

—FREDERICK MARYAT

*"Persistence and determination
are always rewarded."*

— CHRISTINE RICE

"Champions keep playing until they get it right."

—BILLIE JEAN KING

"As long as there's breath in you, persist!"

—BERNARD KELVIN CLIVE

*"Success is the sum of small efforts,
repeated day in and day out."*

—ROBERT COLLIER

"Talent is nothing without persistence."

—DEAN CRAWFORD

*"A river cuts through rock, not because of
its power, but because of its persistence."*
—JAMES N. WATKINS

*"Failure doesn't have to mean defeat,
unless you allow it to."*
—UNKNOWN

"Paralyze resistance with persistence."
—WOODY HAYES

*"A little more persistence, a little more
effort, and what seemed hopeless failure
may turn to glorious success."*
—ELBERT HUBBARD

*"Mindfulness and persistence
overcome all adversity."*
—UNKNOWN

*"No great achievement is possible
without persistent work."*
—BERTRAND RUSSELL

*"We are what we repeatedly do—
excellence, then, is not an act, but a habit."*
—WILL DURANT

*"The key of persistence opens all
doors closed by resistance."*
—JOHN DI LEMME

*"Slight persistent effort can move you
successfully forward in anything you do."*
—KELLI WILSON

7. Be Personable

No one is useless in this world who
lightens the burdens of another.
—CHARLES DICKENS

To be personable means to be genuine, honest, helpful, and friendly. Being personable means you have a personality that others respond to positively. Traits of personability include being welcoming, polite, empathetic, sympathetic, caring, respectful, interested, and outgoing.

Someone who is personable is also sociable and appreciates interacting with all types of people. The characteristics, attitudes, and actions you project into the physical world around you will in time mold your reputation among the people you deal with on a daily basis, from family and friends to employees and colleagues.

To be personable means that you do the following:

♦ Make everyone around you feel relaxed.

♦ Display empathy, a caring attitude, and a genuine connection with others.

♦ Address people by their name.

- Actively listen to what someone has to say, rather than simply hear their words.

- Use positive verbal responses to show engagement and interest when someone speaks.

- Ask pertinent questions to show attentiveness.

- Encourage people to speak about themselves.

- Create an environment that promotes positivity, laughter, and happiness.

- Encourage those around you to invest in their own personal growth.

- Avoid passing judgment on others.

For teachers, it's imperative to be as personable as possible with students. I learned early on teaching high school students that the difference between those who trust you and those who don't lies in how personable you are with them; the students observe this in the form of how much effort and energy you exert relating to them and getting to know them.

Great educators stand at the door when the bell rings and welcome students individually by name as they come into the classroom. This simple greeting may not seem like a lot, but to many students, such a teacher might have been the first person that day to acknowledge them by name and show interest in their lives, even if all the teacher said was "How are you today, [insert name]?" A great teacher tries to learn as much as possible about all students, finding out their interests and passions, likes and dislikes, all in an effort to better relate to them. A great teacher cares about students' ability to master not only the course curriculum, but also their ability to master their self-improvement, self-awareness, self-motivation, and personal wellness. Great educators recognize when something's off with their students and they aren't themselves, and they offer their time in case the students want to talk about what's bothering them. This personal approach, which creates trust between the student and the teacher, fosters a welcoming environment that is imperative to an effective, engaging, and thriving classroom experience.

What You Radiate

Personable people don't allow their mood, no matter how poor it may be, to negatively affect the people around them. A key to this is understanding the importance of maintaining an upbeat attitude and positive expression when associating with others. You wouldn't want to be the type of person who walks into a room and immediately elicits the question "What's wrong?" from everyone there—would you? Because if that happens, the only possible reason would be your negative body language, which you're projecting to everyone else in the room!

Janet Lane-Claypon, an English physician who pioneered the science of epidemiology, said, "Of all the things you wear, your expression is the most important." It's vital to understand that it's not the newest pair of shoes or coolest new seasonal sport coat we wear that tells people our story. Rather, it is our behavior, choice of words, body language, and facial expressions that paint a picture of us to everyone we meet. Despite the never-ending excuses we make for ourselves—blaming our poor personality traits on our genetics or zodiac signs or anything else we can think of—we most certainly do have the *control* and *choice* to wear a smile every day and positively project ourselves to the people around us, rather than negatively doing so.

Some people are born personable; others have to mindfully and actively work toward *becoming* personable. Personable people make an effort to lift the spirits of those around them instead of putting them down; they notice when someone is out of sorts and needs a listening ear or maybe a hug to let them know that somebody cares for them. I don't believe it's reasonable to expect that you have to be friends with everyone you meet, but you should be friendly and helpful to everyone you meet.

Practicing Your Principles

Sometimes, in order to find out the areas of life we need to improve on most, we must ask those closest to us for an honest opinion. This requires us to place ourselves in a vulnerable position, but in doing so, we position ourselves to grow in a positive direction.

Find people in your life whom you trust—people who can be impartial, objective, and honest—and pick one to start. Ask that person if they have any suggestions as to how you could become more personable. Listen to their responses and apply their advice to your daily life to help you become an improved version of yourself.

WORDS OF THE WISE
ABOUT BEING PERSONABLE

*"It's nice to be important, but it's
more important to be nice."*
—JOHN TEMPLETON

*"Students don't care how much you know
until they know how much you care."*
—JOHN C. MAXWELL

*"You will never influence the world
by trying to be like it."*
—SEAN MCCABE

*"You cannot dream yourself into a character;
you must hammer and forge yourself one."*
—JAMES A. FROUDE

*"Every time we push personal development aside,
we invite personal struggle into our lives."*
—HAL ELROD

*"The greatest gift you can give to somebody
is your own personal development."*
—JIM ROHN

*"Kindness is a language which the deaf
can hear and the blind can see."*

—MARK TWAIN

*"Your energy introduces you
before you even speak."*

—UNKNOWN

8. Choose Your Perspective

You have your way. I have my way. As
for the right way, the correct way, and
the only way, it does not exist.

—FRIEDRICH NIETZSCHE

Perspective is a particular attitude you have toward something; it is the subjective evaluation of your environment, your point of view. A positive perspective helps you make better decisions, create new mindsets, make improvements, solve problems, and complete tasks at a high rate of success.

Perspective is based on your beliefs, experiences, environment, health, upbringing, etc. It's based on the pair of lenses through which you view your world. These lenses are the combination of all sensory stimuli and mental experiences unique to *you*, which then mold and shape your perceptions of the world around you.

One of the most intriguing aspects to perspective is that two people can observe a situation from the same visual viewpoint, but process it from two very different mental perspectives. We often hear reports of two witnesses to a crime who viewed the same phenomena but from two different perspectives—resulting in different accounts. Both of these perspectives may be technically correct; they're just relative and subjective, seen through the eye of the beholder.

Any long-lasting relationship or marriage will undoubtedly have conflict at points throughout its duration. Such conflicts or arguments sometimes stem from differing opinions and perspectives. *Some* of these conflicts are necessary in order to grow emotionally closer with one's partner; however, oftentimes, there is a bull-headed, self-righteous attitude that shouts, "I'm right, you're wrong!" This can be incredibly toxic for both people. Such negative conflicts will continue within a relationship/marriage until each partner is willing to relate and empathize with the other person's perspective, thus achieving mutual respect.

When you're having a disagreement or argument with someone, it's helpful to empathize with the individual and attempt to see things from their perspective, in order to better relate to their perception. It's also important to note that in *any* argument, with *any* person, you cannot allow yourself to react negatively and become angry, mad, or jealous over someone disagreeing with you. Your perspective is *yours*, and if other people disagree with you or have a perspective different from your own, then that is OK!

It takes a trained mind not to allow other people's differing perspectives to evoke emotional, knee-jerk reactions in you that make you desperate to prove you're right and they're wrong. Only argue your perspective to someone if you can do so cordially, and when you and your debater are both committed to helping each other see something new, rather than converting each other to your own *one true way.* Do not argue your perspective simply to prove your point or be purposefully argumentative—it will exhaust you and tax your personal wellness heavily.

Learning "Proper Perspective"

On my 16th birthday, I was informed that I'd be getting the hand-me-down family car, a 1994 Ford Escort station wagon. I was excited to finally be driving, but to be honest, I was initially a bit disappointed. After all, I went to a public high school where it was typical for kids to drive new Cadillacs, Corvettes, Mustangs, BMWs, and everything in between. I had a feeling of being "lesser" because I *chose* to compare myself to other people in the school parking lot who drove cooler machines than the one I had.

This self-pitying perspective plagued me until I met a fellow in my 11th grade math class. He was a senior who worked 40-hour weeks as well as being a student, and he walked or rode his bike to all of it. He didn't have a car, so he worked all those hours to save enough money so that he could afford a vehicle and avoid all those sweaty bike rides in the Florida heat.

I was ashamed of myself, but it was an important learning moment. Immediately, my perspective changed as I realized how thankful I should be that I even had a car! On top of that, how grateful should I have been that I had a vehicle that not only got me from point A to point B, but that also allowed me to ferry my friends along with me wherever I was going. The initial embarrassment I felt from my old hand-me-down car was necessary so that I could learn to practice gratitude and form a better perspective—to understand how fortunate I was.

Life provides two unique opportunities. When it becomes cumbersome, "unfair," negative, and toxic, you can sulk in ill temper and pout in aggravation, *or* you can exercise "proper perspective" and learn how to turn the negative situation into a positive one. Disappointments are temporary if you do your best to be mindful and practice proper perspective. When you do this, your frustrations and regrets will slowly dissipate.

The Power to Choose

One of the most amazing gifts a human being possesses is the *power to choose*! Sadness and disappointment do not have to be eternal. If you're going through continued discontent and dissatisfaction in your life, then you need to change your environment, reevaluate your purpose, and begin thinking with a different perspective.

One summer, I was out with a friend and his dad fishing, and after catching loads of fish, we decided to call it a day. We brought the boat in, got it on the trailer, and headed to a deli for a bite to eat, in celebratory fashion. When we got to the deli, I noticed a homeless couple seated in the parking lot asking for money. I felt bad for them and wondered if my buddy's dad would give them anything. My friend and I lagged behind his dad as we walked in, and from a short distance I saw that he conversed with the homeless but didn't give them anything. From my perspective, I thought my friend's dad was in the wrong for not helping them.

Once in the deli, my friend asked his dad why he hadn't given them anything. He told us that when he walked up to them, he offered to buy them *each* a sandwich, snack, water, and even some assorted toiletries. Rather than show gratitude for the generous offer, they had replied that they'd rather be given money. He told us that sometimes, the money you hand to someone who's in that position may not go toward necessities like food and water, but rather toward something unnecessary, perhaps even to fuel an addiction.

After telling me his perspective, I realized my initial judgment had been improper. Once I *listened* to his side of the story, I realized I had previously judged my friend's dad too quickly, and that my previous perspective had been wrong.

Choosing to look at things with the right perspective requires self-training, mindfulness, and practice. Through the practice of proper perspective, you can turn something you initially perceived as a negative into a positive. To make the choice to be mindful and practice proper perspective takes time, effort, and energy. But once you do, you'll see positive effects in many different areas, and you'll have a noticeably more optimistic and happy disposition.

Ultimately, *practicing* proper perspective to change negatives to positives will no longer be necessary because what once disrupted your positivity and mental well-being will no longer have any effect on you whatsoever. So much of your happiness depends on how you choose to look at the world. This choice and perspective affects all aspects of our life. The more practice you put into exercising proper perspective, the more positivity, encouragement, and personal wellness will come into your life.

Practicing Your Principles

Try always to be conscious of your perspectives. Proper perspective isn't something that happens overnight; it is an active practice that you have to be aware of at all times in order to maintain your personal wellness. Having the ability to see others' perspectives and better relate to them is also imperative to your becoming a more understanding person.

For example, think of a time you were stood up by somebody. Maybe you asked them on a date and they said no. Rather than think there was something wrong with you, or that you were inadequate, choose instead to have the perspective that the person who stood you up wasn't right for you and was missing out on all of the amazing things you have to offer. This helps to improve your own confidence and image of yourself, all through the power of choosing the right perspective.

WORDS OF THE WISE ABOUT CHOOSING YOUR PERSPECTIVE

"Complain because the rose bush has thorns, or rejoice because the thorns have roses."

—ALPHONSE KARR

"A clever person turns great problems into little ones, and little ones into none at all."

—CHINESE PROVERB

"Try to see things differently—it's the only way to get a clearer perspective on the world and on your life."

—NEAL SHUSTERMAN

"Injuries give you perspective; they teach you to cherish the moments that I might have taken for granted before."

—ALI KRIEGER

"A weed is but an unloved flower."

—ELLA WHEELER WILCOX

"To change ourselves effectively, we first have to change our perceptions."

—STEPHEN R. COVEY

"The voyage of discovery consists not in seeking new landscapes, but in having new eyes."

—MARCEL PROUST

"Your reality is as you perceive it to be. So, it is true, that by altering this perception we can alter our reality."

—WILLIAM CONSTANTINE

"When you realize there is nothing lacking, the whole world belongs to you."

—LAO TZU

"A man sees in the world what he carries in his heart."

—JOHANN WOLFGANG VON GOETHE

"I am convinced that life is 10% what happens to me and 90% how I react to it."

—CHARLES R. SWINDOLL

"The moment you change your perception is the moment you rewrite the chemistry of your body."

—DR. BRUCE H. LIPTON

"Minds are like parachutes—they only function when open."

—THOMAS DEWAR

"I have always believed that the light at the end of the tunnel is not an illusion; the illusion is the tunnel itself."

—SAM HARRIS

9. Participate in Philanthropy

I have found that among its other benefits,
giving liberates the soul of the giver.

—MAYA ANGELOU

Philanthropy is the effort and desire to increase the well-being, prosperity, and welfare of mankind through charitable acts. It means offering your services, energy, money, or whatever other gift you can give someone, with the understanding and conviction that you won't get anything in return. When you hear the word *philanthropy*, extravagant ballrooms filled with tuxedos and fine gowns may come to mind. However, philanthropy does not have to be extravagant, as all it really requires is for you to make your best effort and intention to improve the quality of life for someone else. When you perform a benevolent and generous act for another person, you're being philanthropic.

I wholeheartedly recommend watching a documentary directed by Roko Belic called *Happy* (2011). It thoroughly discusses and analyzes the science of happiness, as assorted people from around the world are interviewed on the topic. The last person interviewed in the film is a German man named Andy Wimmer. As a former banker, Wimmer acquired an immense amount of wealth and lived a posh and expensive lifestyle. But at some point, he began to feel that something was missing from his life, something incredibly important he had yet to experience.

Wimmer soon met someone affiliated with Mother Teresa's Kalighat Home for the Dying Destitutes in Calcutta, India. The man suggested that if Wimmer came to the Home and volunteered his time and energy for the sick and dying, he might find what he was seeking.

On one of Wimmer's first days volunteering in Calcutta, a young boy who had been found in a garbage dump was brought in. Wimmer held the boy and tried to help feed and nurture him. The boy eventually opened his eyes and made eye contact with Wimmer. Reflecting on the experience, he said in the documentary, "But then he opened his eyes and looked at me, and I thought, *So that's it now*. It was like a flash; it was like a small enlightenment. You learn a lot from these patients we care for. For example, acceptance and tolerance also . . . . To show them that they are loved by God, that they are not forgotten, that their life is precious, that someone cares . . . . There's a tremendous sweetness in taking someone's burden off a little bit. Just to lift this little bent body and take their burden away a little bit and help them to carry it . . . . You serve your brother in front of you who is in need, and it gives yourself a fulfilled, happy life . . . perfect, no?"

Selflessness

Selflessness is a quality of any true philanthropist; it means practicing your philanthropy for the *correct* reasons. Doing something for the sole purpose of making someone else notice you is *not* a healthy habit. Being philanthropic so that others can gawk at you over a donation or contribution completely defeats the purpose of doing something genuinely for another person with the right intention.

We live in an age when, due to the influence of social media, people are doing kind, philanthropic things—*but only* in an effort to get more likes, comments, and subscriptions. Now, people who are given a generous gift in the form of a free meal or a handful of cash certainly aren't going to complain. However, people who perform philanthropy are living a lie if the only reason they help a person is to record it, put it on Instagram, and inflate their ego and image of themselves from the attention they receive thereafter.

People should be generous and benevolent to *all* people, not because they're being watched or because someone may leave a "like" on their Facebook page, but because they have integrity and they know that they're doing things with *right intention*. Living with integrity and doing things with the right intention is paramount to happiness, purpose, and personal wellness.

Philanthropy does not require excessiveness, like giving a crisp $20 to every person you see, but rather a constant willingness to help everyone and anyone in *whatever form* you can. Only the privileged few are able to sit at $500-per-plate events, dancing the night away and bidding on extravagant vacations, with all proceeds going to charity.

This picture is not a common reality for 99 percent of people living on this planet, as most barely have enough to get by day to day. So what do you do to be philanthropic if you're not made of money?

For starters, you can live with compassion! Give your time to others, be selfless, be empathetic, be kind, and contribute to others' comfort and well-being! This alone is our purpose as people; can you imagine a world where people mindfully lived to give more to others than what they take from them? To offer more to people, animals, and the environment than what is expected in return is the ultimate form of philanthropy. If everyone did this, the entire world would benefit overnight.

Years ago, I frequented a grocery store where lots of homeless folks congregated. My friends and I often saw an older woman, probably in her late fifties or early sixties, who would sit under the shade of a palm tree in the parking lot with a sign that said, "Anything helps." One day after seeing her, we walked into the store, took care of what we needed to get, and then, at one of our group's suggestion, began to compile a gift bag of essentials for her. This included a toothbrush with a hygienic cover, some toothpaste, a gallon of water, some toilet paper, a bag of pretzels, and a sub from the deli.

After paying, we walked out and there she was, still under the palm tree. The look in her eye after being handed the bag of goodies was the only reward we needed, as it gave us genuine feelings of happiness and compassion. The shock on her face made it apparent to us just how much it meant to her that strangers wanted to take a little time to care for her and lighten her burden that day.

Try to do something like this at least once a month; each time, you'll experience a new level of self-fulfillment and compassion that will propel you to your next great state of personal wellness.

Random Acts of Compassion

My experience with the woman from the grocery store inspired me to come up with the phrase and practice of Random Acts of Compassion: things you do for other people that are thoughtful, helpful, and positive. I try to perform at least one Random Act of Compassion every month, while continuing to live by the philanthropic principles discussed in the previous section. When people invest in others, they immediately feel a positive and invigorating energy from their thoughtfulness, and the person receiving the Random Act of Compassion is filled with immense gratitude for the love, compassion, and concern that someone has shown them.

Curtis Jenkins is a school bus driver for Lake Highlands Elementary School and the Richardson Independent School District in Dallas, Texas. Curtis lives his truth every single day he goes to work, by being an indispensable part of the lives of the many children that ride his bus. He doesn't see himself as just a bus driver, but rather as a man who commits himself entirely to the growth and personal wellness of each child he's responsible for on a daily basis.

Like any good educator, Curtis not only learns the children's names, but also shows he really cares by finding out their interests, hobbies, and goals. Curtis even made the effort at Christmas to play Santa Claus for all of the kids who rode his bus, wrapping more than 70 presents for his young commuters and giving specialized gifts to each student.

Curtis Jenkins's philanthropic deeds leave a lasting impression of benevolence and love on the children he cares for; the children will remember Curtis and his generosity for the rest of their lives, and his acts of compassion will encourage them to pay it forward and look out for others in their future, the way he looked after and cared for them.

Another wonderful example of a random act of compassion comes from former NFL football player Travis Rudolph. When Travis was a student at Florida State University, his football team attended an event at a middle school, where Travis noticed sixth-grader Bo Paske sitting alone at lunch. Travis decided to sit and eat with the boy, and the two became fast friends. Shortly thereafter, the story of the two went viral.

A Random Act of Compassion is something that you do spontaneously for a complete stranger. I mentioned empathy, kindness, and compassion as philanthropic qualities; however, a Random Act of Compassion entails gifting a stranger something—whether it be cash, food, water, or (as with Travis Rudolph) time. A Random Act of Compassion goes past the day-to-day kindness and compassion you should express toward people naturally; this is going the extra mile, going out of your way to make someone's day—someone who otherwise would never have interacted with you.

The Dalai Lama of Tibet said, "If you want others to be happy, practice compassion; if you want to be happy, practice compassion." This is one of the truest statements that you can live by and strive to practice as a principle of life. Philanthropic deeds will help fulfill your happiness needs. Doing well for others, helping others, being generous to others, and practicing compassion for others are of paramount importance to live well and achieve personal wellness.

Practicing Your Principles

Find time this week to be philanthropic. Maybe the opportunity will come when you're picking up your morning coffee and you decide to pay for the person behind you. Maybe you'll notice your older neighbors' trash cans need to be brought back up to their house. Perhaps the story of making a gift bag for the homeless resonated with you, and you'll decide to go that route.

You could get a street scraper or trash-picking tool and help pick up cigarettes and loose trash around town, taking pride in providing a cleaner environment for your community. In this sense, you'll not just be serving other people, but you'll also be serving Mother Earth herself. Another option is to go to your local Humane Society or animal shelter to volunteer your time with kittens and dogs who have nobody. You could even sponsor a handful of the animals until they find homes; that way, the animals won't be put down. Whichever route you choose to take, do your best to perform some act of philanthropy as frequently as possible.

WORDS OF THE WISE
ABOUT PHILANTHROPY

*"Those who are happiest are those
who do the most for others."*
—BOOKER T. WASHINGTON

*"The best thing to do with the best
things in life is to give them away."*
—DOROTHY DAY

*"The best way to find yourself is to lose
yourself in the service of others."*
—MAHATMA GANDHI

"You've got to give more than you take."
—CHRISTOPHER REEVE

*"Remember that the happiest people are not
those getting more, but those giving more."*
—H. JACKSON BROWN, JR.

*"The wise man does not lay up his own
treasures. The more he gives to others,
the more he has for his own."*
—LAO TZU

"Giving opens the way for receiving."
—FLORENCE SCOVEL SHINN

"You have never really lived until you have done something for someone who can never repay you."
—JOHN BUNYAN

"We must give more in order to get more."
—ORISON SWETT MARDEN

"Giving is the master key to success, in all applications of human life."
—BRYANT MCGILL

"No one is useless in this world who lightens the burdens of another."
—CHARLES DICKENS

10. Live with Poise

Balance is not something you find,
it's something you create.

—JANA KINGSFORD

To live with poise means to live with balance. A poised life is a state of being in which equilibrium, stability, and balance are achieved and maintained in all aspects of life. Attaining poise is not easy, as it requires time, practice, and patience. So much is expected of the modern individual in a capitalistic society: daily responsibilities of family, work, bills, and social friendships/relationships that require consistent attention—not to mention the private aspect of life that should receive the *most* attention and care: the time spent enjoying one's passions, helping others, and reflecting inwardly to work on oneself.

When you achieve and maintain poise, you'll notice an exceptionally positive change in your life: more happiness, more peace of mind, more serenity, and a greater sense of self-fulfillment and self-achievement. To live a poised life means that you're flexible, willing to adapt to new challenges, willing to change old habits when necessary, and willing to *go with the flow* when required. All of these variables in life are proof that poise is not a single, one-time achievement, but rather a lifelong, never-ending practice.

To achieve poise, you have to spend an adequate amount of time and energy maintaining each aspect of life, including family, occupation, hobbies, friendships, etc. If at any point, you feel guilty about not giving enough time to one or more of these aspects of life, then you're not living in balance. When this happens, regain poise by reevaluating the amount of time you're spending on each responsibility.

As their kids become adults, many parents reflect on their time as a family and regret not having spent as much time with their children as they would have liked. Perhaps they spent too much time working at their job, partying with friends, posting on Facebook, or engaging in personal hobbies, rather than spending time with their children. But people who live a poised life avoid this issue by appropriately and proportionately spreading out their time, prioritizing what matters, and assuring that they spend enough time with their children to provide a nurturing and encouraging environment. This present, "in-the-now" poise eliminates the chances of future regret.

Consider today's educational environment. Grades are very important to students and parents. Parents want to make sure their kids are staying on top of their work, and in the ultracompetitive world of modern education, young students undergo an incredible amount of stress. Eventually, their socialization and personal development begin to suffer; as they spend more and more time with their heads buried in textbooks, they spend less and less time outside with friends, exploring and being kids. The best parents recognize when their children hit this point, and they begin to reorganize the children's schedule in order to help them find more poise. With their time better prioritized, the children have an opportunity to enjoy life more and find more happiness, while still maintaining good grades.

Keys to Inner Poise

Achieving poise in relation to the inner self is an art all its own. The keys to inner poise are *self-awareness, introspection,* and *the ability to control your reactions.* These themes are imperative for self-growth and inner balance. When you attain inner poise, bountiful benefits manifest in your inner and external life as well; in other words, internal poise translates into success in the outer physical world in which we live.

Self-awareness means being conscious of your character, feelings, wants, desires, motives, and actions. It means having a clear understanding of your strengths and weaknesses, accepting your positive *and* negative personality traits, and understanding that opinions and beliefs are relative and unique to every individual. The late, great self-growth author and life coach Debbie Ford said, "Self-awareness is the ability to take an honest look at your life without any attachment to it being right or wrong, good or bad."

Yet how many of us can detach from our ego and take an honest and objective look at ourselves? How many of us can reliably reflect and discern between the good and bad behaviors, thoughts, and actions we partake in? Furthermore, how many of us are willing to make the necessary change to rectify what we find? Achieving this state of self-awareness pertains directly to our ability to be introspective, the next key.

Introspection is the analysis and review of your conscious thoughts, feelings, and beliefs. Introspection can make you a more caring, sympathetic, and empathetic human being. It requires cultivating silence, an art that is far too rare in the modern age of constant sensory stimuli. People don't like silence—it requires them to think and acknowledge their subconscious, and it requires self-awareness. In today's world, whether people are stopped at a red light, waiting to be seen in a doctor's office, or standing in line at the grocery store, they are usually on their phones. If they're not on their phones, they're grabbing for some mind-numbing entertainment magazine. With so many stimuli, both from the phone and advertising, there is less and less time for introspection, and it is very noticeable today. Only when *introspection* and *self-awareness* become part of people's daily regimen can they really begin to become poised.

Another key to achieving and maintaining poise is the *ability to control reactions*—reactions to what someone says or does and reactions to naturally occurring inconveniences. Whether they are famous people from reality TV or politicians in Washington DC, the media and entertainment industries depict an endless number of embarrassing, self-destructive, knee-jerk reactions people have when they don't get what they want. It may not even be that they don't get what they want, as much as they don't hear what they want to hear. Or they may feel the need to air their disagreements over things they believe they are correct about. In this case, when people disagree over what they believe to be true, they automatically become upset, distraught, and enraged.

The issue here is that all people see life through their own two eyes—experiencing this life through their own perspective—and there will be an endless number of times when someone's perspective is different from yours. And that's OK! Ethnicity, nationality, upbringing, and culture all affect the way people perceive the world around them. Therefore, it's an unintelligent response to allow yourself to be affected negatively by someone who disagrees with your beliefs and perspectives.

As we discussed in Chapter 8, by allowing people with a contradictory perspective to affect you negatively, you're giving them immense power over you. Don't give them this power! Despite the common excuses such as "that's just who I am" or "I can't control how I feel," you absolutely do have control over your reactions, your feelings, and yourself. It takes endless practice to "quiet" your ego and to not react to people with differing opinions, the way they want you to. They want to debate! They want you to admit that you're wrong and they're right! Why play their game? Staying true to yourself and your feelings does not have to include playing other people's argumentative games and the egotistical back and forth of "who's right." Even when people hurt you with their words and actions, you have the power to ignore their words and build up a wall of your own self-love, which won't allow for their actions or words to affect you in a negative way. This is poise.

Conquering life's "inconveniences" also falls within the category of learning how to *control our reactions*. It embarrasses me to reflect on how often I've gotten angry while driving. Whether it was because someone was driving too slowly, or I got stopped by a train on my way to work, or the traffic was just bad in general, I would end up angry. I still struggle with this, if I'm being completely honest.

However, I reached a new level of poise in my life when I finally stopped allowing these very minor inconveniences to play a very large role in my day. If I'd left for work at an appropriate time, the train and traffic wouldn't have bothered me. It's not the train's fault I'm late, it's my own!

Bruce Lee well understood the importance of limiting emotional reactions to others, as he stated, "You will continue to suffer if you have an emotional reaction to everything that is said to you. True power is sitting back and observing everything with logic. If words control you, that means everyone else can control you. Breathe and allow things to pass."

True power is being faithful to yourself, being true to yourself, and not allowing outside opinions, thoughts, and comments to affect you negatively. People live their entire lives allowing every little thing that happens to evoke an emotional reaction in them—what an exhausting way to live! Mastering your reactions to others will propel you toward an eternally poised life.

Practicing Your Principles

Are you a poised person? Do you feel like everything in your life is in proper balance and harmony? Or do you feel as if you're being pulled in too many directions, unable to be attentive to the things that matter most? Evaluate the time you're spending in the different areas of life and reflect honestly on what you can immediately start doing differently to attain more composure and poise.

WORDS OF THE WISE ABOUT POISE

"The key to winning is poise under stress."
—PAUL BROWN

*"Man maintains his balance, poise, and sense
of security only as he is moving forward."*
—MAXWELL MALTZ

*"Self-esteem is a matter of balance. Too much
can tip over into haughtiness, arrogance, and the
inability to admit when we have gone wrong."*
—ALAN SCHMIDT

*"Live a life that is well balanced;
don't do things in excess."*
—DANIEL SMITH

*"Balance is a feeling derived from being whole
and complete; it's a sense of harmony."*
—JOSHUA OSENGA

*"It is the same with people as it is with
riding a bike. Only when moving can one
comfortably maintain one's balance."*
—ALBERT EINSTEIN

"Happiness is not a matter of intensity but
of balance, order, rhythm, and harmony."
—THOMAS MERTON

"Poise is power."
— FLORENCE SCOVEL SHINN

"Be moderate in order to taste the
joys of life in abundance."
—EPICURUS

"Remember that poise and power are inseparably
associated. The calm and balanced mind
is the strong and great mind; the hurried
and agitated mind is the weak one."
—WALLACE D. WATTLES

"The critical part of a balance in
life is choosing priorities."
—BYRON PULSIFER

"Next to love, balance is the most important thing."
—JOHN WOODEN

ii. Possess Confidence

*Because one believes in oneself, one doesn't
try to convince others. Because one is content
with oneself, one doesn't need others'
approval. Because one accepts oneself,
the whole world accepts him or her.*

—LAO TZU

Possessing confidence refers to your capacity to strongly
believe in yourself, as well as your ability to positively
handle various situations, complete challenging tasks, attain
self-goals, and achieve new friendships. Confident individuals don't concern themselves with what other people do as
the *norm* or *standard*. People who possess confidence generally take "the path less followed" and are more inclined to
act differently from everyone else in the crowd.

Confident people don't rely on reassurances and affirmations from other people; rather, they assert themselves
into positions of leadership and establish their own customs,
emitting an irreplaceable energy that draws other people
to them. Those who possess confidence don't worry about
what other people might think of them: they dress how

they want to dress, speak how they want to speak (without offending or hurting others), and believe what they believe, all in accordance with *their own* truth.

Remember that there is always a fine line between possessing confidence and being arrogant, which is why it's imperative to be attentive and self-aware enough to avoid unintentionally offending or hurting someone. In order to possess confidence and avoid arrogance, you must avoid arguing for the sake of arguing and realize you don't have to get in the last word. We looked at this in Chapter 8 on perspective and again in the previous chapter on poise, but it's worth repeating: confident people express their opinions but aren't offended when someone disagrees with them, while arrogant people *are* offended when someone disagrees with them and continues to argue. Along with taking offense at those who disagree with them, arrogant people will continue to dispute their opinion and argue their personal perspective as if it were the only truth.

Going with Your Gut

One fundamental of possessing confidence concerns the phrase "go with your gut." As a high school teacher, I've shared this old adage with my students more often than any other. Nearly every time a student changes an answer after completing a question, the new answer is wrong and the original answer was correct. But "go with your gut" is not an ideology to be associated only with scholastic endeavors; people in general have a very difficult time going with their gut, especially if it's connected to cutting toxic people out of their life.

In Chapter 2, we talked about letting go of toxic relationships as part of forgetting the past. Going with your gut can be helpful in such cases because, whether dealing with a bad relationship or a friendship that's run its course, many of us are unwilling to take the next step and cut toxicity from our lives. We don't possess the confidence to cut out that toxicity and recognize that we'll be better off without it.

Anytime you have to cut ties with someone who was once special to you, that sick feeling in the pit of your stomach starts to form. Pay attention! That feeling is your subconscious letting you know that something's not quite right in your association with that person, that things aren't the way they used to be. This then indicates that you must take some new action to calm your distress. If the problem still exists after taking time to try to mutually fix it, then it is the proper time to "go with your gut" and end that affiliation, in order to stop spending energy and time on a person who's no longer good for you.

Other Keys to Confidence

Possessing confidence also means being OK *spending time alone*. Of course, it is important to be social with family and to have positive friendships, but positive time spent alone is just as essential. Bruce Lee said, "A wise man can always be found alone. A weak man can always be found in a crowd." Don't seek out validation and affirmation from those in "the crowd"; rather, possess confidence and be certain enough of yourself to be comfortable alone.

"To be yourself in a world that is constantly trying to make you something else is the greatest accomplishment."

With this, Ralph Waldo Emerson articulates the importance of self-reliance, uniqueness, originality, and individualism. You must possess confidence to reach the level of self-care and self-love Emerson is alluding to. When you choose to be wholly yourself, with all the quirks and oddities that come with that, you put yourself in a vulnerable position. This vulnerability means being open to criticisms and critiques from "the crowd" while realizing that what "the crowd" says or thinks about you is *none* of your business because it doesn't pertain to who you really are.

A monumental amount of freedom comes to someone who *doesn't take anything personally*. Who cares what another person thinks of your shoes or your points of view, which are unique to *you*? Don't waste a second of your energy validating your thoughts and actions to people in "the crowd." Instead, possess the confidence not to take anything personally and push away any words and actions from others meant to negatively affect your happiness and wellness.

Stop comparing your life to that of everyone else around you. Ignore what others are doing with their lives because ultimately, it should have no effect on the life you live. Instead, possess confidence to live your own unique journey, one that makes you happy, motivated, and fulfilled. In order to propel yourself to the best you, you must possess the confidence to break the limits you've set for yourself, to outgrow old bad habits, and to make the absolute realization that *you* are your only competition in life. As a people, we spend all this time comparing ourselves to complete strangers, but the truth is that the only thing you've got to compare yourself to is you! Every day should be dedicated to outshining yesterday's you, not other people.

Practicing Your Principles

Choose something you've always wanted to participate in but never have because you lacked the confidence to do so. Make this activity your new goal and learn as much as you can about it in order to possess the confidence to give it a try, even if you don't do as well with it as you'd initially like.

WORDS OF THE WISE ABOUT CONFIDENCE

"Doubt kills more dreams than failure ever will."
—SUZY KASSEM

"Always be yourself, express yourself, have faith in yourself; do not go out and look for a successful personality and duplicate it."
—BRUCE LEE

"Stand up for what you believe in, even if that means standing alone."
—ANDY BIERSACK

"Never mind what others do; do better than yourself, beat your own record from day to day, and you are a success."
—WILLIAM J. H. BOETCKER

"You can succeed if nobody else believes it, but you will never succeed if you don't believe in yourself."
—WILLIAM J. H. BOETCKER

"Whether you think you can or think you can't, you are right."
—HENRY FORD

"A man cannot be comfortable without his own approval."
—MARK TWAIN

"Confidence comes not from always being right, but from not fearing to be wrong."
—PETER T. MCINTYRE

"You yourself, as much as anyone in the entire universe, deserves your love and affection."
—SIDDHARTHA GAUTAMA, THE BUDDHA

"As soon as you trust yourself, you will know how to live."
—JOHANN WOLFGANG VON GOETHE

"Don't be satisfied with stories, how things have gone with others. Unfold your own myth."
—RUMI

12. Maintain Physical Well-Being

The first wealth is health.

—RALPH WALDO EMERSON

To maintain a state of physical well-being requires you to take proper care of both your body and your mind. Physical well-being requires a focus on fitness, food, mindfulness, and learning, as well as the fortitude to tie it all together into a lifelong practice. Achieving and maintaining physical well-being should be one of the most important priorities in your life—especially since your personal wellness depends on it.

Below is a guide to help you maintain a perpetual state of physical well-being.

Ten Habits of the Healthiest

1. Eat nutritionally dense foods, with focus on a wide variety of fruits, vegetables, beans, seeds, legumes, nuts, and wild-sourced animal proteins. Always try to buy local.

2. Drink clean water daily. Avoid soda, energy drinks, caffeine, and alcohol as much as possible.

3. Practice proper hygiene to avoid common illnesses.

4. Get enough sleep.

5. Meditate and look inward for personal reflection and self-discovery.

6. Learn yoga, which helps to increase flexibility and strength, protects from injuries, and improves respiration, energy, and vitality.

7. Practice moderation and avoid excessiveness.

8. Write out and plan meals for the week to avoid last-minute trips to a fast-food joint.

9. Participate in some form of aerobic exercise, whether it be running, cycling, hitting a punching bag, or playing a team sport.

10. Participate in some form of resistance training, whether it's with old-school barbells or the modern-day, easy-to-use machines.

Preventing Heart Disease—Our #1 Killer

The National Center for Health noted in November 2018 that heart disease was the leading cause of death in the United States from 2016–2017, followed by cancer. The president of the American College of Cardiology, Dr. C. Michael Valentine, MD, FACC, said, "Nearly half of all Americans have high blood pressure, high cholesterol, or smoke—some of the leading risks factors for heart disease—but these are often either preventable or modifiable risk factors that we can all work to reduce. While we are constantly finding innovative ways to treat existing heart disease, we must continue to focus our efforts on preventing heart disease. It will require efforts not only from just the medical community, but from communities and governments as well. Saving our hearts is a problem we must solve together."

It's hard to believe that this has quickly become the new normal way of life, and it has become evident that each individual will have to take an active part in educating themselves and their loved ones in order to avoid this deadly trend. Widespread sickness from heart disease and general heart-related problems is a relatively recent occurrence; for most of human history, those diseases were lumped together as the "diseases of kings" because the only people who could monetarily afford to eat themselves sick were royalty. If you look back at famous commissioned paintings of royalty from Europe, generally speaking, the royal is rather large.

In the book *The Pleasure Trap* (2006), authors Douglas J. Lisle, PhD, and Alan Goldhamer, DC, write, "Periodic feasting on calorically dense foods did not constitute a problem for hardworking farmers and tradesman, still struggling to get enough. But for the power elite, the possibility of continuous feasting led to the appearance of a new set of diseases—heart attacks, strokes, congestive heart failure, diabetes, hypertension, obesity, arthritis, gout, and cancer. These diseases, often described as the illness of affluence or the 'diseases of kings,' are now the leading causes of death and disability in the industrialized world." The authors go on to say that throughout history, these disease conditions—the diseases of dietary excess—were almost exclusively reserved for the wealthy class, as animal and processed foods remained expensive delicacies.

As the Industrial Revolution transitioned into the twentieth century, new comforts and luxuries— including the ability to feast endlessly on unhealthy foods—became available to more and more "average," everyday individuals. From the milkman delivering bottles to the front door to the opening of the original modern grocery store, life became more and more convenient and comfortable. With this convenience came the decision to eventually have manicured yards with hedge bushes and flowers, rather than edible food; less cultivation of food from home led to the endless encouragement to go to the grocery store and buy all sorts of foods and goods that have no positive effect on human health, and generally hurt more than they help.

Today's "get-fit-quick" diets aren't sufficient for a lifetime of great health. Sure, noticeable weight loss may result in a short period of time, but it isn't proper weight loss and it's not realistic to maintain. The diets may promote high protein and high fat or maybe high protein and low fat; however, most of them lack sufficient nutrition, which requires antioxidants, protective phytochemicals, vitamins, and minerals to keep us healthy. That's why it's best to do your own research to find the most nutrient- dense foods that exist on the planet and find a way to get a great variety of these nutritionally dense foods into your body as often as possible.

Dr. Joel Fuhrman, MD, author of countless food and nutrition books, says in his book *Super Immunity* (2011),

"The combination of high-nutrient intake and low-caloric intake promotes disease resistance and longevity. It is the basis for my health equation: Health = Nutrients/Calories." White flour, simple sugars, and processed foods as a whole have become the foundation of the average American's diet, while fresh fruits and vegetables, seeds, nuts, and beans have been neglected and put on the back burner. It isn't a matter of opinion or subjective interpretation—it's a fact. Dr. Fuhrman goes on to say, "Incredibly, by 2010 these processed foods had become 62 percent of the calories in the standard American diet." The human body reacts differently to different foods, and some foods offer us innumerable amounts of nutrients and minerals, while others offer absolutely *zero* nutritional benefits. In fact, in addition to providing no health benefits, they have scores of negative side effects that can impact the body with catastrophic health consequences.

Treat Your Body Like a Rolls-Royce

In high school, one of my close friends competed for the state swimming championship. He was only 17 years old and was in incredible shape; he dieted, exercised on his own, and had a precise regimen that he followed daily. On the other hand, I was a fat young musician with no athleticism and *zero* understanding of my body and the basic principles of health that rule it. I asked my friend to give me some inspiration, to offer me any perspective that might encourage me to take a path toward achieving physical well-being.

He said, "Imagine you own a Rolls-Royce. Would you

put cheap regular fuel in it, or would you put in the best premium gas money can buy?" I promptly replied that I'd use premium gas, as it would obviously allow the vehicle to run optimally. He replied, "My body is like a Rolls-Royce. I don't want cheap fuel—junk food; I only want premium— nutritionally dense foods rich in vitamins and minerals." This simple metaphor was life changing for me, as it eventually helped me begin my personal quest to become healthier and more responsible with my food and exercise choices.

When you go to the grocery store, you're given an incredible amount of responsibility and choice. You can buy an array of decadent and tempting snack food, or you can fill your shopping cart with real foods that will make you thrive. When you begin to treat your food like a medical checklist, as opposed to something that gives your brain pleasurable inputs, your health will inevitably get better. The same goes with the conscious decision to work out and exercise or to stay stagnant and lazy.

Socrates said, "It is a shame to grow old without seeing the beauty and strength of which the body is capable." You owe it to yourself to create the best version of your body possible, within the realistic limits of your abilities. Whether or not you want to compete in sports or include weekly exercise as part of your life's ritual, it is imperative to exercise regularly to help position yourself for a long life of health and personal wellness.

Practicing Your Principles

Put your physical well-being at the very top of your priorities list. It is imperative that you apply yourself toward better understanding the food you consume and your body's reaction to aerobic exercise, weight training, and team sports. By applying yourself, you will turn into the best physical specimen that you can be. Look over the Ten Habits of the Healthiest in this chapter and assess those you're applying and those you need to work harder at. Despite how much you can learn on your own, always talk to your physician before making drastic changes to your routine.

WORDS OF THE WISE
ABOUT PHYSICAL WELL-BEING

"Physical fitness is the first requisite of happiness—in order to achieve happiness, it is imperative to gain mastery of your body."
—JOSEPH PILATES

"To keep the body in good health is a duty—otherwise, we shall not be able to keep the mind strong and clear."
—SIDDHARTHA GAUTAMA, THE BUDDHA

"The secret of good health lies in successful adjustment to changing stresses on the body."
—HARRY J. JOHNSON

*"A healthy body is a guest-chamber for
the soul; a sick body is a prison."*
—FRANCIS BACON

*"To ensure good health: eat lightly, breathe
deeply, live moderately, cultivate cheerfulness,
and maintain an interest in life."*
—WILLIAM LONDEN

*"Wellness is the complete integration of
body, mind, and spirit—the realization that
everything we do, think, feel, and believe
has an effect on our state of well-being."*
—GREG ANDERSON

"A healthy outside starts from the inside."
—ROBERT URICH

*"Take care of your body. It's the
only place you have to live."*
—JIM ROHN

*"Physical fitness is not only one of the most
important keys to a healthy body, it is the basis
of dynamic and creative intellectual activity."*
—JOHN F. KENNEDY

*"The reason I exercise is for the
quality of life I enjoy."*
—KENNETH H. COOPER

*"If you don't make time for exercise, you'll
probably have to make time for illness."*
—ROBIN SHARMA

*"When it comes to health and well-
being, regular exercise is about as close
to a magic potion as you can get."*
—THICH NHAT HANH

*"True enjoyment comes from activity of the mind
and exercise of the body; the two are ever united."*
—WILHELM VON HUMBOLDT

*"Reading is to the mind what
exercise is to the body."*
—JOSEPH ADDISON

*"The root of all health is in the brain. The
trunk of it is in emotion. The branches and
leaves are the body. The flower of health
blooms when all parts work together."*
—KURDISH PROVERB

13. Position Yourself for Success

*The best preparation for tomorrow
is doing your best today.*

—H. JACKSON BROWN, JR.

To properly position yourself means making a conscious effort to place yourself in the best situations and circumstances possible, as well as setting short-term and long-term goals. "There's no such thing as good luck, only good positioning" is something my dad's been telling me since I was a kid.

My father was my hockey coach for quite a few years. Anytime we lost and the team was bummed out, he'd say that quote matter-of-factly. If someone complained about the refs or said the other team got lucky against us, he'd simply say, "No, they outworked you and they positioned themselves to win more than you guys did." And he was right!

This lesson applies not only to traditional schooling through college, but it goes all the way to the professional world. To position yourself for increased positivity, success, self-growth, and prosperity, you must have proper *preparation* and *planning*.

To be *prepared* is to be properly equipped and ready in advance for something to yield as much positive productivity as possible. You accomplish this by physically and/or mentally being engaged with something ahead of time. Proper *preparation* is especially important when responsibilities such as tests, presentations, performances, or championships occur.

To *plan* means to formulate a scheme or program for the accomplishment or attainment of a specific aim, purpose, or goal. To best attain and then maintain something, create a *plan* and put it into writing. It's not enough for it to be in your head; put it on paper or a dry erase board to help you stick to the *plan* and manifest the end goal.

Mindful positioning helps increase personal wellness in a number of ways. Positioning helps you stay focused, become more organized, progress to success more easily, prioritize responsibilities, and free up time in the future by taking care of things in the present.

Here's a good example. I give my tenth-grade world history students a study guide before every test. If they actively listen to lectures, take notes, participate in their classwork, and properly study before a test, they will undoubtedly do well in my class. It's a recipe meant to help them succeed scholastically. But only they can make the choice to follow the recipe. Even though I give all my students an elaborate and complete blueprint for scholastic success, some refuse to properly position themselves.

For the longest time, it bothered me that I couldn't convince *all* my students to want to do well, even though

I gave them a strategy for success. I needed to change my perspective, and I soon realized that even if I encourage *just one* student to do better—not only to get an A on my French Revolution test, but to do better at life in general—then I can feel I've succeeded as an educator.

Setting Goals for Positioning

Positioning for short-term goals consists of dedication to a daily regimen that is devoted to near-immediate achievement, whereas positioning for long-term goals pertains to increments of small change that become noticeable over time. A short-term goal could be, "I want to gain five pounds of muscle in the next two months," while a long-term goal might be something like, "I want to triple my financial wealth over the next five years."

To achieve such goals, you have to position yourself in their direction. Many people know what they want, but they aren't willing to position themselves for it because of the work that it entails. If you want to put on five pounds of muscle, you're going to need to adjust your caloric intake, spend tons more time at the gym, and begin pursuing new knowledge pertaining to muscle growth. If you want to triple your income, you need to begin positioning yourself for higher paying jobs, entrepreneurial pursuits outside your main income, side jobs, etc.

November 2017 was when I first started performing live music as a side job from teaching, and it was initially very new and very stressful. It was only stressful because I was trying to learn how to master and put on the best solo acoustic set possible; playing saxophone in a band my whole life was far different from this new form of musicianship. I played a few shows here and there, but early on, I didn't get booked often.

Then the manager of a local restaurant where I had been trying to play finally got back to me and booked me for a gig a couple of weeks later. The manager told me if the gig went well, I'd be a regular. Finally, I had the opportunity I was looking for! I made a mental note and a screenshot of the text so that I had the date saved in my phone. Unfortunately, it turned out that was not adequate positioning, and those lazy couple of steps were not good enough reminders: I forgot about the gig and missed it. When they called me, I was already a half-hour late, and they told me to forget about it and that maybe they'd call me again someday—which they never did.

I had struggled with organization my entire life and had never really taken any serious steps toward fixing the problem, but missing that gig taught me that if I wanted to be a more successful musician—and adult in general—I'd have to start positioning myself better. The first thing I did to position myself for more success and no more forgetfulness was to buy a calendar dedicated strictly to my music gigs. It paid off, as I've never missed a gig since.

Wake up every day and ask yourself, What will I do today to position myself for more personal success in my life? Whether it requires more *planning* and *preparation* to accomplish your goals or a necessary change of environment to avoid certain people and temptations, you have the power to position yourself in any direction of success you wish; you just have to be willing to put in the necessary effort and energy to see it manifest. One of the most important yet difficult lessons you can learn in life is that no one owes you anything—literally, nothing. But you owe yourself everything. Start positioning yourself *now* in order to attain everything you want in the future.

Practicing Your Principles

Position, prepare, and plan your life so that you are able to accomplish everything you want to achieve. Short-term and long-term goals require a plan of action and a dedication to positioning yourself in whatever direction(s) your ultimate objectives and passions lie. Think of some short-term and long-term goals that you want to set for yourself. Put them in writing, look at them and read them every day, and begin accomplishing your goals.

WORDS OF THE WISE ABOUT PROPER POSITIONING

"A man who does not plan long ahead will find trouble at his door."
—CONFUCIUS

"Opportunity does not waste time with those who are unprepared."
—IDOWU KOYENIKAN

*"He who is best prepared can best
serve his moment of inspiration."*
—SAMUEL TAYLOR COLERIDGE

"A goal without a plan is just a wish."
—ANTOINE DE SAINT-EXUPÉRY

*"Proper positive positioning is the
key to experiencing miracles."*
—EDMOND MBIAKA

"By failing to prepare, you are preparing to fail."
—BENJAMIN FRANKLIN

*"Planning is bringing the future into the present
so that you can do something about it now."*
—ALAN LAKEIN

*"Before anything else, preparation
is the key to success."*
—ALEXANDER GRAHAM BELL

*"Proper planning and preparation
prevents poor performance."*
—STEPHEN KEAGUE

*"Plan for what is difficult while it is easy;
do what is great while it is small."*

—SUN TZU

*"Success is where preparation
and opportunity meet."*

—BOBBY UNSER

*"Setting a goal is not the main thing—it is
deciding how you will go about achieving
it and staying with the plan."*

—TOM LANDRY

*"For tomorrow belongs to the people
who prepare for it today."*

—AFRICAN PROVERB

*"To accomplish great things, we must not only act,
but also dream; not only plan, but also believe."*

—ANATOLE FRANCE

*"Men succeed when they realize that their
failures are the preparation for their victories."*

—RALPH WALDO EMERSON

14. Praise Others and Show Gratitude

Gratitude is the most exquisite form of courtesy.

—JACQUES MARITAIN

To offer praise means to express warm approval and strong admiration for someone or something. Gratitude is the appreciative awareness and thankfulness you offer people in response to kindness or assistance they give you. I cannot overstate the importance of expressing praise and gratitude in your day-to-day life. Unfortunately, the hustle and bustle of the average day can lead to tons of stress and impatience, likely preventing you from offering mindful praise and gratitude to those around you who assist you and are a part of your day-to-day existence.

Anyone who helps you over the course of your day, from the barista taking care of your 7:00 a.m. coffee order to the person who holds the door an extra five seconds for you, deserves praise. Of course, there are varying levels of praise, the most common expression being "thank you." Saying "thank you" to someone who's done something for you is of course the right thing to do, but there's something you can say to make it even more personal, which will express your gratitude even further. Instead of saying "thank you" to people, begin telling them, "I appreciate you." The latter is a more personal way to offer praise and a more distinct way for you to positively affect their day.

You don't have to offer compliments and praise only when someone does something nice for you; in fact, anytime you offer praise, you have a positive effect on someone's day. Ruthie Lindsey, author of *There I Am* (2020), believes "If you see something beautiful in someone, speak it"—and this is exactly the theme I'm talking about. Every day, you have the power and ability to make people's day a little brighter by offering them a compliment and praise. You learn that a coworker has just received an award? Congratulate them. You notice people are looking a little more trim and fit? Praise them for it and tell them you're proud of their change! Your neighbor in the office cubicle is reading a new book? Inquire about it. Although we should never seek praise, we should look for every opportunity to offer it in hopes of making other people's day happier and more positive.

Social Media and the Pitfalls of Comparing Yourself to Others

Making the practice of gratitude a habit of life can have tremendously positive effects on other people—as well as yourself. People are so hungry for praise and approval that massive numbers have turned to social media to find it. But this is backfiring in so many ways.

For example, at present, people are relentlessly encouraged by social media's construct of "story modes" to spend lots of time and energy posting about themselves throughout the day; this encouragement leads people to do things during their day they would otherwise never do. That's not to say that it can't be a cool way to share an immediate and unique moment with friends and family *once in a while*, but many people spend their *entire* day recording things to post to a story. If that story mode didn't exist, they'd never be doing half the things they're doing because so much of it is only for their followers—aka their audience—to see.

That's a pretty crazy phenomenon, if you think about it; it's a habit that has only existed since the Snapchat app first introduced its story mode back in October 2013. Countless other social media platforms have since copied the format and created their own version. Even more important than understanding the problem of excessive posting is discussing how all of this creates an environment of constant, never-ending comparisons to one another.

As discussed previously in this book, this persistent judging and comparing can lead to excessive pride, vanity, egotism, and for some, even narcissism. For many people, the constant comparing leads to feelings of self-doubt, sadness, lack of confidence, and sometimes even depression. Do these negative themes just appear from out of nowhere? Of course not—they come from a place of jealousy and envy over seeing people on social media with *more* than they have. More of what, though? The general sentiment is "they've got more 'things' than I do, and theirs are shinier and nicer than mine."

It's easy to begin focusing on the things we don't have. This then leads to a negative view of oneself, along with feelings of sadness and self-pity. Instead of entertaining this kind of negativity, we need to be grateful for the things we do have. There is so much to be grateful for in our lives, and if we train our brain well enough to start being aware of the things we have to be grateful for, we'll never allow ourselves to spend even a second comparing ourselves to others and judging ourselves against the materialistic attainments of others.

Imagine a man is sitting at a stoplight waiting to get to work, when a woman with a new sports car he could only dream of owning pulls up beside him. It's the exact model and color he wishes he had for himself.

As the two cars wait at the light, a bicyclist passes through the intersection in front of them on the way to her job. She looks at the two people inside the cars, comfortably air conditioned and shielded from the exhausting heat she's pedaling in. She can't help thinking to herself, *If only I had a car*, as she continues on down the road.

A few miles ahead, she passes a man waiting at the bus stop who's disabled, missing a leg. When he sees her briskly flying down the street on her bike, he can't help thinking to himself, *I wish I still had my leg so I could enjoy the simpler things in life I used to love, like riding my bike.*

The point is: always be grateful for what you have—you can't imagine how many people hope and wish for the most basic things that we often forget to express gratitude and thankfulness for.

See the Big Picture

Practicing gratitude releases an energy that is not otherwise felt. In the process of reflecting on the *real* things one has to be thankful for, there can only be a sense of appreciation that leads to bright feelings of joy and love.

At the beginning of the school year, I ask my tenth-grade world history students to write down three things they're grateful for; the general responses I get back include "my phone, the internet, Instagram, video games, my new car, etc." Very rarely do they take a step back and look at the innumerable big-picture things they have to be grateful for. This is not their fault, however, as society does not encourage this type of reflection and thankfulness. My hope, of course, is that at the end of the year, when I ask that question again, their responses will reflect different values, as they begin to ponder the more important things to be grateful for in their lives.

This pattern of thinking is not unique to my young students, as I always tell them that people my age and older also struggle with properly expressing gratitude for the things in life that matter most. Many people don't express such gratitude unless encouraged to do so mindfully and on purpose, despite the fact that these are the things that deserve the most veneration and respect.

Do you have a sense of smell, sight, and taste? Seems silly to think about, but when we spend the kind of time and energy on certain things that we do (maybe when something doesn't go our way?), we forget about these seemingly small things. But on second thought, thinking about small but important things shows proper scope and perspective.

Do you have clothes to wear? Are you able to breathe with ease? Is there a roof over your head at night, and does your house have proper heating and air? Do you have somebody in your life who truly cares about you and loves you?

If you lack any of these things, then my deepest sympathies go out to you. But many people have all of these things and don't realize that not everyone does until someone points it out to them. I certainly didn't always feel grateful for the good things in my life; it took me years and many teachers to point me toward this perspective. Ralph Waldo Emerson said, "Cultivate the habit of being grateful for every good thing that comes to you, and to give thanks continuously." When you begin to give daily gratitude for your family, friends, profession, passions, abilities, health, and more, your life becomes a much more enjoyable experience, filled with noticeably more compassion, consideration, and personal wellness.

Practicing Your Principles

To better practice my daily gratitude, I have a dry-erase board I call my "Grateful Board," with the ten top things I'm grateful for. Depending on what's happening in life, this list may change, but generally, there is a consistent theme for the most important things. I keep the dry-erase board on my bathroom counter, and when I first wake up and get ready to shower, I look at my "Grateful Board" and read the ten things. Sometimes, it isn't enough just to read them mentally. To really have them manifest and become real to me, it's necessary for me to read them out loud. It may sound goofy to some people—fair enough. However, I can say that there is a noticeable difference for me when I forget to do this morning ritual, as I'm generally less patient and not as pleasant and friendly.

A Grateful Board might include things like this:

"I'm most grateful for..."

1. My family

2. My friends

3. My abilities

4. My job

5. My purpose

The most basic things we often forget about may also be included on your Grateful Board, such as access to clean water, food, shelter, refrigeration, good health, and use of the senses.

WORDS OF THE WISE ABOUT PRAISE AND GRATITUDE

"Appreciation is a wonderful thing. It makes what is excellent in others belong to us as well."

—VOLTAIRE

"No duty is more urgent than that of returning thanks."

—JAMES ALLEN

"Let us be grateful to people who make us happy; they are the charming gardeners who make our souls blossom."
—MARCEL PROUST

"Gratitude makes sense of our past, brings peace for today, and creates a vision for tomorrow."
—MELODY BEATTIE

"Saying thank you is more than good manners. It is good spirituality."
—ALFRED PAINTER

"Gratitude is not only the greatest of virtues, but the parent of all others."
—CICERO

"Feeling gratitude and not expressing it is like wrapping a present and not giving it."
—WILLIAM ARTHUR WARD

"If you want to turn your life around, try thankfulness . . . it will change your life mightily."
—GERALD GOOD

*"When I started counting my blessings,
my whole life turned around."*
—WILLIE NELSON

*"Too often we underestimate the power of a touch,
a smile, a kind word, a listening ear, an honest
compliment, or the smallest act of caring, all of
which have the potential to turn a life around."*
—LEO BUSCAGLIA

15. Eliminate Pride

In general, pride is at the bottom
of all great mistakes.
—JOHN RUSKIN

The word *pride* has many definitions and interpretations. In the positive sense of the word, pride is a sense of your own dignity or value—your self-respect. It's also the pleasure or satisfaction you take in your work or self-efforts. Upon reaching a personal goal or crossing a finish line in sports, for example, you might be filled with bountiful joy and pride in your achievement. There's absolutely nothing wrong with pride displayed in these contexts. However, there's a negative aspect to pride, expressed as an excessively high opinion of yourself in the form of conceit, vanity, or arrogance. This chapter focuses on this negative aspect and how to overcome it.

It seems today's society is more prideful than ever. This may be the result of its current near-instant gratification system pertaining to electronic gadgets and entertainment or the futile culture of living for "likes." Or perhaps it's because people are divided on so many social and world issues. As a result of this division, people become convinced that their thoughts and their perspective, as viewed through their two eyes, constitute the only truth. And with this self-certainty comes the prideful perspective of "I'm right; you're wrong."

This type of thinking leads to a natural proclivity to judge others for thinking or living differently from the status quo. But one of life's most important lessons is not to judge anyone, and to instead use that energy to constantly focus on self-improvement. With today's distractions and nonstop commotion, it's hard to refuse the self-obsession and pride we're encouraged to live out. Yet refuse them we must, in order to best maintain our personal wellness. We shouldn't take pride in money, social media followers, professional titles, or degrees; rather, we must allow ourselves to live with humility, compassion, integrity, and generosity.

That's not to say that a comfortable financial situation and great education aren't something to be proud of—they absolutely are—but they're not anything to gloat about to others. Take pride in yourself *quietly*.

It's always difficult to see people allow their ego and hubris to interfere with friendships and relationships. When disagreements brew between family and friends, those with too much pride will allow the suffering and anguish to continue because of their ego, rather than put their differences aside in order to find a solution. In college, for example, I allowed a misunderstanding with one of my best friends to affect our friendship for over a year. I was visiting him at the University of Michigan, and after a fun Saturday morning at the football game, we headed back to his apartment to get ready for the night. Somehow, things got mixed up with our plans for the evening, and assumptions were made that left me feeling as if I had been wronged. But rather than solve the issue right then and there, I let my pride take over. My ego decided that my buddy was in the wrong and had done me wrong, and that he and I were no longer on good terms.

The reality is that both of us communicated poorly and there was no real justification for my anger. It took me over a year to handle that situation properly and end up talking it through with my friend. It turned out my assumptions had been wrong and there had been no excuse for my anger; I had allowed my pride and ego to get in the way of a great friendship. So, solve problems when they come up—don't allow your ego and pride to convince you that you're not a part of the necessary solution to the problem.

That Comparing Thing Again

People with a big ego and lots of pride constantly compare themselves to others. As we've discussed previously, comparing one's accomplishments to others' is an unhealthy habit that leads to more self-obsession and further distance from personal wellness. A persistent trait of prideful people is the need to one-up others. Those who thrive on validation will insert themselves into a group setting and butt into conversations to one-up whoever is currently the focus of attention. Being interrupted by someone who is trying to outshine you is incredibly annoying. It's not an easy thing to point out to others; often, they will insist you're being sensitive or that they're just eccentric and you should tolerate them. Those who interrupt and one-up don't realize that they're presenting their insecurities while simultaneously bothering everyone in the group with their rude interruptions.

Pride and egotism are synonymous. People with a corrupted ego have a tendency to speak about themselves excessively, conceitedly, and boastfully. This ego drives a need to be right all the time, a need to argue, and a need for constant attention from others. People with inflated egos thrive on hearing validation from others; it's what helps to perpetuate their prideful behavior.

The reason people need so much reassurance and attention from others these days is that they are not confident and comfortable with themselves without others' validation. To correct their egotism and excessive pride, they must commit to self-reflection and self-assessment of their attitude and behavior. As always, the only real and permanent solution to the problem is going to have to come from within. They alone possess the change they seek.

Practicing Your Principles

Managing our egos and eliminating the destructive behavior that comes from inflated pride is a tough task. It requires the vulnerability of self-reflection and may require us to ask an impartial family member or friend which areas of our life our ego is damaging and influencing in a negative way.

The next time you find yourself arguing with someone, see if you can take a breath before responding again, to really hear what the other person is saying. Instead of trying to prove your point and get in the last word, try saying, "You could be right." Or try the straightforward approach and say something like, "I don't agree with you, and here's why." This takes away the emotional "charge" that the ego loves and lets people know you're committed to real communication rather than being right all the time.

WORDS OF THE WISE ABOUT PRIDE

"There are two kinds of pride, both good and bad. "Good pride" represents our dignity and self-respect. 'Bad pride' is the deadly sin of superiority that reeks of conceit and arrogance."
—JOHN C. MAXWELL

"The quieter you become, the more you can hear."
—RAM DASS

"Behind every argument lies someone's ignorance."
—LOUIS D. BRANDEIS

"It is better to lose your pride with someone you love rather than to lose that someone you love with your useless pride."
—JOHN RUSKIN

"Pride is pleasure arising from a man's thinking too highly of himself."
—BARUCH SPINOZA

"Most of the trouble in the world is caused by people wanting to be important."

—T.S. ELIOT

"Pride is the mother of arrogance."

—TOBA BETA

"If someone corrects you and you feel offended, then you have an ego problem."

—NOUMAN ALI KHAN

"Pride is spiritual cancer: it eats up the very possibility of love, or contentment, or even common sense."

—C.S. LEWIS

"Pride costs us more than hunger, thirst, and cold."

—THOMAS JEFFERSON

"If you get your ego in your way, you will only look to other people and circumstances to blame."

—JOCKO WILLINK

"Your ego is your soul's worst enemy."

—RUSTY ERIC

"When the ego dies, the soul awakes."
—MAHATMA GANDHI

"The ego, however, is not who you really are. The ego is your self-image, it is your social mask, it is the role you are playing. Your social mask thrives on approval. It wants control, and it is sustained by power because it lives in fear."
—DEEPAK CHOPRA

16. Prioritize Your Life

To change your life,
you need to change your priorities.

—MARK TWAIN

We are so busy in today's world with responsibilities and pressures coming from every direction that it is more important than ever for us to prioritize our lives in order to efficiently live to the best of our ability. Anytime we choose between two possible courses of action, we establish our priorities. When we set priorities, we make a statement about what's most important and/or urgent in our life.

A teacher demonstrated a great way to set priorities. She filled a large glass vase with three rubber balls. Then she poured in marbles, followed by a bag of salt and a bag of sugar, until the vase was completely full. She then said to her students:

The vase represents the overall balance of your life.
The three rubber balls represent your physical health,
family, and friends, all of which are irreplaceable. The
marbles represent various responsibilities you'll have

someday, like balancing a checkbook, having a job, being responsible for car payments, pursuing new knowledge, etc. If you fail at, or lose any of these, it's going to be difficult to deal with initially—but disappointment can be overcome and you will inevitably persist. The sugar and salt crystals represent the smaller, sweeter, and more savory things in life, the things pertaining to materialistic pleasures. These can easily be replaced. If you prioritize your life in this order, you will be able to fill your "vase" the best way possible.

Anytime you attempt to make an organized list of responsibilities, wants, and future actions, you are creating your priorities. At some point, you've probably had a good eye roll after hearing the age-old "get your priorities straight!" from a parent or teacher. But . . . they're not wrong. When you prioritize, you stay organized, and with better organization inevitably comes a life of more ease and less stress.

Make a list now. On your list, rank each item in order from the most important priority to the least important. The wisest people tend to prioritize their lives so that the most difficult and arduous work is always at the forefront of the day; by not putting things off, they achieve success and productivity in their day and have time later on for leisure and personal interests. It's also much easier to successfully attain and maintain purpose when purpose is a priority.

I often use scraps of paper to write prioritized lists of errands and tasks that I need to complete for the day. Some people don't like this approach because it's too disorganized; scraps of paper can get lost easily, and they'd rather have a journal or electronic calendar of some sort instead. That's fine! For me personally, ten times out of ten, I lose a journal shortly after purchasing it; whereas, I have surprisingly consistent success at not losing scraps of paper! But whether it's on a scrap of paper or in a journal with your initials embroidered on it, making prioritized lists will keep you more organized, more proficient with your time, and less stressed.

Prioritizing your time at home is important too. It's easy to look down at your phone, start to scroll, blink twice, and then notice suddenly that hours have passed. By prioritizing your time at home, you can have time to do everything you need in order to be your best self. Setting time aside for physical fitness, reading, self-education, cleaning and basic household chores, responsibilities for work, etc., is important to staying your best. When I was a kid, my dad would break down my free time over a weekend almost to the hour: TV time, homework time, study time, outside play time, video game time, etc. I hated it as a kid, but as an adult, I realize that it taught me important life lessons on how to efficiently prioritize my time.

I would categorize time in two categories: *time consumed* and *time devoted. Time consumed* refers to the type of time we devote to watching non-educational television, scrolling through Instagram, partying excessively, being gluttonous, lounging, etc. *Time devoted* refers to time spent learning new skills, finding new passions, reading new books, starting new projects, volunteering for others, or creating a side job where you get to use your talents to earn extra income.

Every day, you get 24 hours; that's 1,440 minutes or 86,400 seconds. This time is nonrefundable, nonrenewable;

you can never get it back. So at some point, we have to have an honest talk with ourselves to decide whether or not we are prioritizing our time wisely. As you evolve, you grow, and part of that growth is becoming more careful with how you use your time.

Practicing Your Principles

Prioritize your life to make time for all the different aspects that need attention. Your prioritized list can include any of the following:

1. Short- and long-term goals

2. Purposes to pursue and maintain in your life

3. Basic errands and tasks

4. Phone calls, time, and energy devoted to maintaining social and family relationships

WORDS OF THE WISE ABOUT PRIORITIES

"It is not a daily increase, but a daily decrease. Hack away at the inessentials."
—BRUCE LEE

"The key is not to prioritize what's on your schedule, but to schedule your priorities."
—STEPHEN COVEY

"Decide what you want, decide what you are willing to exchange for it. Establish your priorities and go to work."
—H. L. HUNT

"The mark of a great man is one who knows when to set aside the important things in order to accomplish the vital ones."
—BRANDON SANDERSON

"Our life is the sum total of all the decisions we make every day, and those decisions are determined by our priorities."
—MYLES MUNROE

"Good things happen when you set your priorities straight."
—SCOTT CAAN

"Lack of time is actually lack of priorities."
—TIMOTHY FERRIS

"The first step to success is knowing your priorities."
—ASPESH

"Times of transition are strenuous, but I love them. They are an opportunity to purge, rethink priorities, and be intentional about new habits. We can make our new normal any way we want."
—KRISTIN ARMSTRONG

"Life is short. Focus on what really matters most; you should change your priorities over time."
—ROY T. BENNETT

"Be OK with what you ultimately can't do, because there is so much you CAN do."
—SAM BERNS

"Nobody's life is ever all balanced. It's a conscious decision to choose your priorities every day."
—ELISABETH HASSELBECK

"We don't drift into good directions. We discipline and prioritize ourselves there."
—ANDY STANLEY

"No one is going to hand you an organizational chart. You have to hand it to yourself."
—ROBERT GENN

17. Project Probity

Before you speak, let your words pass through
three gates: Is it true? Is it necessary? Is it kind?

—RUMI

To live life with probity means living a life committed to complete and confirmed integrity, virtue, and honesty in one's conduct and character. It can be thought of as consciously trying to do all things with the right intention. This high standard of demeanor doesn't pertain to just your interactions with others in public or at work, but it also relates to the way you treat yourself.

There are genuine "right" reasons for doing something, and there are "wrong," deceitful, and dishonest reasons. When we take misleading and deceitful actions for personal gain at the cost of someone else's well-being and happiness, then that personal gain is essentially worthless to us because we did it out of selfishness and not out of integrity and honesty.

Let's look at how this plays out in two areas of life: communication and relationships.

Living Life on Display

One aspect of probity today has to do with our ability to communicate. Despite our "smart" phones being glued to our hands at all times, giving us the ability to communicate with anyone in the world at the press of a few buttons, we are collectively perhaps the worst communicators that have ever existed on Earth. This is not unique to the younger generations—poor communication is affecting everyone.

This is because the smartphone enables and encourages people to live life as if they're their own TMZ. Many people are *obsessed* with taking pictures and recording every minute of their life, to a manic degree. The "likes" and "comments" from their social media posts feed their constant need and hunger for attention in general. It's gotten to the point where people aged 10 to 60+ are exerting energy throughout their entire day with the sole purpose of recording and posting events and activities to their social media platform—then doing the same exact thing for the next platform. As previously pointed out, if it weren't for this technology, they wouldn't be doing a lot of these things throughout the day in the first place because without the technology, they wouldn't have this mobile, personal audience.

Since its inception, the camera was meant to capture special moments in time, to secure a magical moment so it could be remembered for all time in the form of a photograph. Is that what we're doing today? Is that how we view the simple yet incredible ability to take pictures? Are we using the smartphone camera responsibly and with integrity? Or are we using it as a result of our obsession, vanity, or need for attention? Do we overly enjoy, to a scary degree, the dopamine dumps that come from our smartphones' buzzing?

These are questions worth asking, as they reveal to us whether we're living a life of probity or superficiality.

Relationships: A Practice Playground

Be honest with yourself and those you meet with regard to what you're looking for in relationships and friendships. Don't tell someone what they want to hear just to justify what you want from that person, all the while knowing you don't *honestly* feel what you're saying you feel. This isn't truthful or virtuous living. This is the selfish and vain road of life, which is quickly infecting just about everyone, from teenagers and college students to professional working adults and couples.

As you receive more interest and attention from new admirers, you begin to feel more comfortable and start to open up more. Opening up to new people automatically puts you in a vulnerable place as you share more and more of who you are. If your new admirers are dishonest with their real intentions and do not fully communicate what it is they want from you, then you may eventually find that your feelings for them are not as genuine and sincere as they once were. You may end up realizing that these people's intentions could end up costing you *your* happiness and well-being.

Many people don't realize their behavior has been hurtful until the same thing happens to them. I was no different in this regard. I mentioned in Chapter 2 a breakup experience I had that now, in hindsight, I know was *necessary*.

It helped me realize that I'd done something similar to someone I'd once loved, and that I was wrong for handling things with that person poorly. Even though it took years to recognize and understand, the realization was pivotal for me because it helped me become aware of and learn from my mistake.

What I learned from this was that things tend to come back to haunt us if we don't learn to recognize our faults quickly enough on our own—that these happenings are by no means random, but rather pivotal experiences in the timeline of our lives that are meant to teach us lessons. The negative karmic consequences of our actions sometimes take the same form as negative experiences we've put others through. Whether or not you mean to affect someone negatively, it is up to you to have enough self-awareness and understanding of *your own intent* to avoid acting selfishly and hurting someone.

The first "agreement" in Don Miguel Ruiz's book *The Four Agreements* (1997) says, "Be impeccable with your word." This means don't speak poorly, negatively, or nastily about other people or yourself. Instead, do the opposite. In your relationships and friendships, speak encouragingly, lovingly, and inspiringly. After all, if you could make a person's day better, wouldn't you want to? You can with the way you speak to others.

The direction of your integrity and moral compass is directly intertwined with what happens to you in your life. As you begin to live with an awareness of this, it will soon become apparent that life happens *with* you, not *to* you. You are responsible for your own life, and your behaviors, intentions, and decisions inevitably affect its outcome.

The more you use your words and voice to put people down, chastise, compare, and overly judge, the more negativity and overall unhappiness you will bring to your life. But the better you carry yourself and the more honesty and integrity you show others, the more you will live with probity, the better your life will be, and the more personal wellness you'll attract.

Practicing Your Principles

Reflect on the power of your words and honestly assess how you speak to others and the intentions you have toward others. Are they honest and up-front? Or are they perhaps a bit deceiving at times? Name one area of your life in which you perhaps have not been as honest as you could have been, and see if you can begin to change this. Realize that by living with more integrity and honesty, you allow better opportunities and circumstances to open up to you.

WORDS OF THE WISE ABOUT PROBITY

*"Every intention sets energy into motion,
whether you are conscious of it or not."*

—GARY ZUKAV

*"The greatness of a man is not in how much
wealth he acquires, but in his integrity and his
ability to affect those around him positively."*

—BOB MARLEY

"Have the courage to say no. Have the courage to face the truth. Do the right thing because it is right. These are the magic keys to living your life with integrity."
—W. CLEMENT STONE

"As long as your intentions are solid and about growth and progression and being productive and not being idle, then you're doing good in my book."
—FRANK OCEAN

"One of the truest tests of integrity is its blunt refusal to be compromised."
—CHINUA ACHEBE

"A good intention is like the seed of a tree whose fruit we do not know."
—GEORGE BERNARD SHAW

"Integrity is the seed for achievement. It is the principle that never fails."
—EARL NIGHTINGALE

"Intention is the core of all conscious life. Conscious intention colors and moves everything."
—HSING YUN

"Leading with integrity and empathy requires vision and a connection to your deepest self."
—KARLA MCLAREN

"Integrity is doing the right thing, even when no one is watching."
—C. S. LEWIS

"Honor your commitments with integrity."
—LES BROWN

"True heroes are made of hard work and integrity."
—HOPE SOLO

"Image is what people think we are; integrity is what we really are."
—JOHN C. MAXWELL

18. Find Your Purpose

The two most important days in life are the day you
are born and the day you discover the reason why.

—MARK TWAIN

Your purpose is any objective or goal toward which you direct effort and energy. Your purpose is something that makes you feel special, something that you care for deeply, something you want to maintain in your life. It is the objective or goal toward which you strive.

Your purpose is something that:

1. Is meaningful and rewarding.

2. Is a pivotal source of motivation.

3. Is intriguing and interesting.

4. Defines you and your existence.

5. Makes you think to yourself, "I'm meant to do this."

People whose goal it is to become a doctor do so because they believe that becoming a medical doctor is their purpose and calling in life. It is too difficult an undertaking to just commit to on a whim. However, before attaining that final goal, their purpose will first have to be to become full-time, dedicated, and hardworking students. Years upon years of very difficult higher education, along with residency, await aspiring students. But if they make their schoolwork their purpose, they will succeed in it. No matter how difficult and intense those responsibilities are, students will master them if they are focused and committed to doing so.

A friend of mine went to her teacher for advice. She said she didn't know what the point of life was or what her purpose was. The teacher said that, in her opinion, life was all about helping others—and she encouraged the girl to volunteer with a nonprofit organization called Best Buddies, which assists people with intellectual and developmental disabilities. The joy and fulfillment my friend felt after her first time volunteering made her quickly understand the lesson her teacher was trying to show her. It was a defining moment because it helped her discover her purpose and calling in life, which was to be an Exceptional Student Education (ESE) educator.

Purpose Changes

Your purpose will change throughout your life, depending on the chapter you're in. For instance, when you're a young professional, finding a job driven by your passions, which we talked about in Chapter 1, is of the utmost importance and gives you the most meaning at that stage of life. However, imagine your life as a retiree and it's easy to see how different your purposes might be at that point, compared to all those decades earlier as a young professional. By that later point in life, you may have had a long, happy marriage full of kids and grandkids, leading you to a new perspective that you simply could not have recognized and a meaning you could not have experienced as your younger self.

Another example is that of retired athletes. When an NHL hockey player retires from the game, it's imperative for him to find a new purpose. Why? Because going to the rink and playing hockey is all he's known since the time he first laced up his ice skates. And when it's officially out of his life, he has to find new purpose in order to continue living happily and well.

Today, many former NHL players, including Darren McCarty, Riley Cote, and Ryan VandenBussche, have found purpose in bringing awareness to current and former players of the medical benefits cannabis can offer professional athletes as an alternative to the dangerous opioids they may currently use for pain management. They've seen firsthand the dangers of opioid abuse, which can lead to vicious addiction, depression, and sometimes even suicide. With their new purpose, these former NHL players try to help improve the quality of life of those around them through their own belief in and applications of medicinal cannabis.

Other players, both past and present, have found new purpose by allowing themselves to discuss their own struggles with mental illness and depression, in order to make it more normal for players to gain the necessary confidence to come forward and seek help if they're struggling. Such sharing requires them to be extremely vulnerable, which is especially difficult to do coming from a hard-nosed hockey background. Former NHL players like Theo Fleury have dedicated their life after hockey to bringing awareness to mental wellness. Even current NHL goaltender Robin Lehner has used his platform as a professional athlete to break down the stereotypes and roadblocks preventing his colleagues from seeking out the help they need to improve their mental health.

If you'd asked any of these individuals as younger men if this would be their life after pro hockey, I imagine their overwhelming response would've been "no." The point is that all of us, even pro athletes, will most likely find new purpose as our lives progress. The key is to trust the direction life takes us during times of change, and to never compare newfound purposes to old ones.

When Money Equals Purpose

Many people make the mistake of making their purpose in life to make as much money as possible. I'm not saying financial freedom shouldn't be a goal in your life—it absolutely can be. However, allowing making the most money possible to be *the* purpose of your life is going about it the wrong way and will likely lead to unhappiness. Instead, find the thing that makes you tick and the unique skills and traits that bring you fulfillment, and then leverage those things in a way that brings about financial success. You might not even need a nine-to-five job to accomplish this!

Many people take a job right out of college related to their bachelor's degree, and they almost immediately hate it. Yet most stay. Why? They stay for the money and the security. But your life and existence should be more than living for Friday and Saturday nights. Every day should make you as happy as you feel looking forward to your weekend. There should be no distinction between a Monday and a Saturday.

The risk that people run by making the accumulation of money the sole purpose of their being is that it *can* lead them into a very vain and materialistic existence. Their obsession with vanity and materialism leads to perpetual unhappiness because their appetite for the newest and best only gives brief happiness; it can never be perpetual. Within months, the next new release will come out, and their most recent purchase will seem worthless. Buying the newest things will give people brief, fleeting releases of dopamine—which are essentially worthless because they're temporary. These extrinsic rewards do not provide people with real meaning and fulfillment. So make it a goal to seek intrinsic rewards rather than extrinsic ones, and in the process, you'll begin to find your purpose.

Purpose gives meaning to human beings, but it is not just given to us. The unhappiest people are those who know they have a purpose inside them but refuse to act on and acknowledge it—because they're so comfortable with the current state of their life, even if it's monotonous, that they fear the uncertainty that comes with taking risk.

It is your responsibility to work effortlessly at improving yourself in order to uncover and discover *your own* exclusive and incomparable purpose(s) in life. There is no limit to the number of purposes you may have, and oftentimes, they may interact and correlate in some way. Whenever possible, engage in your purposes in order to exercise your inner strengths and invoke your passions.

Every new purpose you discover along the way will require you to formulate a fresh and unique game plan to accomplish and maintain it. To find your purposes in life, you have to try new things, be open to having new experiences, and be willing to put yourself in vulnerable positions. Always seek to attain and maintain purposes, both old and new.

Practicing Your Principles

Do you know what your purpose is? Are you living your purpose? If you said no to either of these, take some time to reflect on and determine what you care deeply about. Then write it down and take one step toward adding it into your life.

WORDS OF THE WISE ABOUT PURPOSE

*"Efforts and courage are not enough
without purpose and direction."*
—JOHN F. KENNEDY

*"Good luck is another name for
tenacity of purpose."*
—RALPH WALDO EMERSON

*"Never work just for money or for power. They
won't save your soul or help you sleep at night."*
—MARIAN WRIGHT EDELMAN

"Everyone has been made for some particular work, and the desire for that work has been put in every heart."

—RUMI

"To begin to think with purpose is to enter the ranks of those strong ones who only recognize failure as one of the pathways to attainment."

—JAMES ALLEN

"The purpose of life is to discover your gift. The work of life is to develop it. The meaning of life is to give your gift away."

—DAVID S. VISCOTT

"The mystery of human existence lies not in just staying alive but in finding something to live for."

—FYODOR DOSTOYEVSKY

"You cannot teach a man anything; you can only help him find it within himself."

—GALILEO

"The best way to lengthen out our days is to walk steadily and with a purpose."

—CHARLES DICKENS

"If you bring forth what is within you, what you bring forth will save you. If you do not bring forth what is within you, what you do not bring forth will destroy you."

—GOSPEL OF THOMAS

"You must first be who you really are, then do what you need to do, in order to have what you want."

—MARGARET YOUNG

"The purpose of life is not to be happy. The purpose of life is to matter, to be productive, to have it make some difference that you lived at all."

—LEO ROSTEN

19. Pursue Knowledge

If you have a garden and a library,
you have everything you need.

—CICERO

Pursuing knowledge is the process of seeking wisdom, gaining new experience, and taking the time and energy to learn something new. It's a never-ending process that can yield many wonderful outcomes: it can build your confidence, create new opportunity, enrich your life, help you make better decisions, or allow you to reach a new level of self-growth. Pursuing knowledge also leads to self-liberation, by helping you constantly acquire wisdom and seek truth.

Here are some of the ways I recommend that you pursue knowledge:

1. Ask questions and actively listen.

2. Intern at a job that relates to something you want to do.

3. Investigate the mysteries of life that fascinate you.

4. Read books that cover an array of information and research.

5. Review qualified media sources.

6. Request help from an educator, trainer, or master of the knowledge you seek.

7. Try new things.

Over the last century or so, society as a whole has abandoned the refined and distinguished ways of learning from long ago; today, the cherished study room of the past, filled with books and manuscripts, has evolved—at least for men—into the modern "man cave," full of liquor advertisements and sports memorabilia. I'm not saying it's bad to enjoy sports; I'm a die-hard Detroit Red Wings hockey and Michigan Wolverines football fan, and I look forward to their respective seasons every year.

However, there's a difference between watching a favorite team play from time to time and spending excessive amounts of time watching Sports Center every day, debating with friends over their favorite sports pundit's views, or scanning the hottest fantasy football trends. Modern sports, for the most part, have replaced the love of and respect for the pursuit of knowledge that people had in the past. Enjoy your sports teams, but don't allow your brain to be filled up with unnecessary sports trivia; pick up a book and retrain your brain.

Through training, practice, and study, you can continue to learn for as long as you wish. As you continue your self-education, be sure to seek out reputable and reliable sources. Even if you *think* a source is trustworthy, it is entirely your responsibility to verify anything that you hear or read, even when it comes from a boss or teacher.

Remember, the best way to know if you have truly learned something is to test yourself by trying to convey it to somebody else.

Learning Just for the Love of It

Don't pursue knowledge because you need to; do it because wisdom is truth and liberation! Educate yourself because the knowledge you learn can never be taken from you. Pursue knowledge because you want to learn, because you *know* it enriches your life, and because you know it will help you to grow. The more you learn and the more you continue to commit yourself to pursuing knowledge, the more opportunity you will begin to unlock for yourself. Knowledge really is power; it is the destroyer of mental bondage and the liberator of ignorance.

My Grandpa Lou was the first person who taught me to regard self-education and the pursuit of knowledge as an elixir of life. He told me that pursuing knowledge is "like drinking from the fountain of youth," telling me that if he had ever won the lottery and hadn't had to earn an income to provide for his family, he would've been a professional student for life, studying formally at universities and in the privacy of his study and his personal library.

New knowledge keeps the brain young, active, excited, and eager for self-discovery. I did not understand what my grandpa meant until I reached the age of 26, as I began pursuing knowledge pertaining to new interests and passions of mine, reading book after book and listening to lecture after lecture online in my pursuit of truth. It became an entirely new part of my daily life: scouring books and taking notes in the hope of greater self-fulfillment and a fuller understanding of life.

As you continue to pursue knowledge, you will inevitably discover new interests and passions. Each one of us has our own quest for knowledge to embark on. The knowledge I want to pursue will be different from that of everyone else, and vice versa. There is no single right course in properly mapping the road to liberation through the pursuit of knowledge and self-education.

Many parents today force their kids to complete things like reading and learning before allowing them to have any kind of "fun" (e.g., watching cable television, using their smartphone, playing video games). Children now have a negative view of books and learning. But parents can instill in their children the idea that learning and education are exciting and stimulating—and can transform them into whatever they want to be when they grow up.

Pursuing knowledge will always lead us to new discoveries, regardless of how we gain that knowledge. For instance, dedication to learning from books is of the utmost importance, as books are incredible teachers. But so is learning through exploration and travel to new places. When we travel, we take ourselves out of our comfort zone, allowing ourselves to open up to new experiences. We can't travel to faraway places and act as we would in our homeland—it's necessary to adapt and practice the customs of that place. The active and mindful adaptation and practice of others' customs is an extremely fulfilling form of pursuing knowledge. By expending the energy to understand faraway people and cultures, by learning their way of life, we build character and empathy that we'd never be able to get from reading a book.

Practicing Your Principles

Seek knowledge anywhere you can! Don't limit yourself to the things you're classically trained in from your area of study in high school or college; rather, look for new knowledge outside those areas to achieve a new level of intelligence. The library has historically been the place you'd go to teach yourself something new, and though it is still a great option, the internet has recently revolutionized the ability to self-teach. It has many of the books you'd find in a library, but also manuals and instructional videos, tools that help visual and kinesthetic learners in a way that books can't always provide.

You may have no understanding of cars, but if your brake light goes out, you can watch a video online that will teach you how to fix it yourself. Taking that action saves you money, and over time, that money adds up. Whether it's teaching yourself basic chemistry, learning a new language, or teaching yourself how to play an instrument, challenge yourself to always learn new things in order to become a wiser and better-rounded person.

WORDS OF THE WISE
ABOUT PURSUING KNOWLEDGE

*"Self-education is, I firmly believe, the
only kind of education there is."*

—ISAAC ASIMOV

"Live as if you were to die tomorrow.
Learn as if you were to live forever."
—MAHATMA GANDHI

"I don't believe in colleges and universities. I
believe in libraries because most students don't
have any money. When I graduated from high
school, it was during the Depression and we had
no money. I couldn't go to college, so I went to
the library three days a week for 10 years."
—RAY BRADBURY

"The secret of education lies in respecting the pupil.
It is not for you to choose what he shall know,
what he shall do. It is chosen and foreordained
and he only holds the key to his own secret."
—RALPH WALDO EMERSON

"Many who are self-taught far excel
the doctors, masters, and bachelors of
the most renowned universities."
—LUDWIG VON MISES

"Formal education will make you a living;
self-education will make you a fortune."
—JIM ROHN

"You can never be overdressed
or overeducated."

—OSCAR WILDE

"If you are willing to be a self-learner,
you will develop yourself."

—LAILAH GIFTY AKITA

"I know of nothing more inspiring than that
of making discoveries for one's self."

—GEORGE WASHINGTON CARVER

"There is no wealth like knowledge,
no poverty like ignorance."

—ALI BIN ABI THALIB

"Knowledge is like a garden; if it is not
cultivated, it cannot be harvested."

—AFRICAN PROVERB

"Instead of buying your children all the
things you never had, you should teach
them all the things you were never taught.
Material wears out but knowledge stays."

—BRUCE LEE

"The only person who is educated is the one who has learned how to learn and change."

—CARL ROGERS

"I'm for truth, no matter who tells it—I'm for justice, no matter who it is for or against. I'm a human being first and foremost, and as such, I'm for whoever and whatever benefits humanity as a whole."

—MALCOLM X

20. Make Progressive Resolutions

I think in terms of the day's
resolutions, not the years'.
—HENRY MOORE

Progressive resolutions are personal acts of determination that promote positive change, adjustment, and improvement in your life. Progressive resolutions are not limited *only* to goals that pertain to physical change, such as, "I want to lose 10 pounds!"; rather, they are meant to improve any area of life at any time.

Resolutions related to physical change are often observable to your friends and family. They notice you're eating healthier, more nutritious foods, or they see you start regimented workout routines that result in muscle growth and weight loss. However, non-physical progressive resolutions—matters pertaining to inner improvement or development, purpose, and happiness—are themes not as obvious to friends and family at first.

For example, while losing 10 pounds requires you to exert an incredible amount of *outward* energy, in the form of aerobic exercise or lifting weights, resolving to better control your anger requires you to make an *inward* exertion of energy. In this case, the progressive resolution is only going to come from an inward exploration, with the intention of producing more self-awareness and self-control to better govern your anger—it won't come in the form of dietary change and a gym pass. But no matter what your current progressive resolution pertains to, you need to act on it in order to achieve steady movement and constant improvement.

I once met someone who, upon discussing our mutual interests, I found happened to be a big hockey enthusiast. He had been an exceptional ice skater at a young age and was soon playing competitive hockey. He never had goals of becoming a professional hockey player, but he loved the game. Then, when he was 15, he broke his leg in a freak accident. His life became a carousel of endless doctor's appointments, extreme pain, and feelings of "why me?"

As he continued to lose strength, he understandably fell into depression. Out of fear for his mental well-being, his mother brainstormed with him to find a progressive resolution that would help him with his depression. They decided that since he'd be stuck in bed a while, maybe learning how to play guitar would be a great goal to set. She challenged him to use the guitar as a release of energy from the disappointment of the accident and suggested that setting goals would help pass the time as he recovered.

The broken leg eventually healed, and he rejoined his teammates on the ice. But the accident that had initially left him the most broken he'd ever been eventually led him to discover his incredible guitar ability and musicianship.

His passion for playing hockey would pass as he got older, but his love for music never ceased, and at the time I met him, his daily profession was teaching music lessons. The challenge his mother gave him would turn out to lead to his most important purpose and passion as an adult.

Not Just for the New Year

As a society, we've been hoodwinked into associating the necessary energy needed to make *real* change in our lives with just one time of the year: New Year's. As the holiday season comes to an end in December, the realization hits us that the big bright ball in Times Square in New York City will soon be dropping in front of millions on national television. And rather than look for positive self-improvement and positive change every day, we generally don't think about it, at least in a serious sense, until the end of the calendar year.

Then, suddenly and excitedly, as if the opportunity magically appeared out of pure void, thoughts of self-improvement, progress, and "I really want to be better with ____, ____, and ____ in my life" begin to manifest. We behave as if these seemingly obvious personal issues were sudden developments, rather than a long-standing accumulation of matters we have struggled with for an extended period of time. Yes, it's a positive that we're willing to make change, but why wait until January 1?

As we begin to plan our New Year's resolutions, the themes are generally more of the same: "No more alcohol during the work week, gym five times per week, better diet, read more books, watch less TV, etc." And the twenty-first century is a unique time in which, even if someone we know seems genuine and committed to their New Year's resolutions, we're left to wonder, are they even doing it for the right reason? Are they doing it truly to be a better version of themselves? Or is there a chance that it's not genuine, that the change is coming from a place of vanity—they're doing it to gloat, post, and boast on their social media to show their followers all of the *amazing* improvements they're making.

Along with this, New Year's resolutions almost always pertain to the outward physical improvement of the body, as opposed to inner self-improvement. There's no excuse not to persistently try to overcome obstacles to the outer and inner work at *all* times of the year, in the form of progressive resolutions.

Therefore, always be open enough with yourself that you can acknowledge areas of life that need improvement from *you*. Yes, from *you*! By allowing yourself to be vulnerable and honest, you will receive the ultimate prize, which is self-awareness about the things that need improvement in your life. Set progressive resolutions for yourself as often as necessary in order to continue reaching the last ceiling you set for yourself—whether it's the need to be more thankful, to curse less, to check in on friends more, or to lose those 10 pounds before summer bathing suit season. Don't allow your ego to put it off any longer—be your best, now!

Practicing Your Principles

Do you truly believe you can change your circumstances at any time? Are you certain enough of yourself that you trust that change is eternal, that it is a daily school of thought, and that you can become better in the areas of life that you want? If you don't believe these things, you need to change your perspective because the truth is that you create the conditions that exist in your life. If you want to make great change(s), identify what it is that needs to be worked on, and start now! No need to wait until New Year's Eve—commit to your daily change(s) today in order to have a better tomorrow.

WORDS OF THE WISE
ABOUT PROGRESSIVE RESOLUTIONS

*"A good resolution is like an old horse,
which is often saddled but rarely ridden."*
—MEXICAN PROVERB

*"The secret of change is to focus all of your energy
not on fighting the old, but on building the new."*
—DAN MILLMAN

*"Nothing relieves and ventilates
the mind like a resolution."*
—JOHN BURROUGHS

"A resolution to avoid an evil is seldom framed till the evil is so far advanced as to make avoidance impossible."
—THOMAS HARDY

"I made no resolutions for the New Year. The habit of making plans, of criticizing, sanctioning, and molding my life is too much of a daily event for me."
—ANAÏS NIN

"You're as strong as your resolutions!"
—ISRAELMORE AYIVOR

"If you don't like something, change it. If you can't change it, change your attitude."
—MAYA ANGELOU

"He who is firm and resolute in will molds the world to himself."
—GOETHE

"Write it on your heart that every day is the best day in the year."
—RALPH WALDO EMERSON

"Just because the dates change, does not mean you have to change. The continuous path toward self-improvement is a timeless process."
—BRITTANY BURGUNDER

"Most people will passively do exactly what they did last year. Whatever you do, don't let that person be you."
—RICHIE NORTON

"Every time you tear a leaf off a calendar, you present a new place for new ideas and progress."
—CHARLES KETTERING

"I learned this, at least, by my experiment: that if one advances confidently in the direction of his dreams, and endeavors to live the life which he has imagined, he will meet with a success unexpected in common hours."
—HENRY DAVID THOREAU

About the Author

John M. Bros was born and raised in South Florida, where he grew up with a love for exploration, fishing, and hockey. He graduated from the University of Central Florida in 2013 with a bachelor's degree in Social Science Education, followed by a year in Thailand teaching English. Since August 2015, he has taught World History back in his hometown.

John enjoys reading and listening to all things pertaining to health, nutrition, history, and homesteading. John has an enormous passion for musicianship—which began at the age of eight when he started playing the alto saxophone, taking after his grandfather, who played in big bands and swing bands. Outside of his love for music, John is also passionate about traveling, trying new foods, and farming.

Made in the USA
Middletown, DE
07 September 2020